FUTURE NOW?

THE ART OF IMAGINATION

KELLY SIMPSON   ERIN CONLAN
SHERYL TORR-BROWN, PH.D

Cover design by Lisa Fisher

Copyright © 2019 Medical Vision Press, LLC (MVP)

All rights reserved. No part of this book may be reproduced or used in any manner without written permission of the copyright owner except for the use of quotations in a book review.

CONTENTS

SECTION ONE: The What and Why of Futuring	v
Introduction	vii
1. Why Future?	1
2. The Past and Present of Futuring	11
3. Create the Pause	27
4. How Your Brain Resists Looking Ahead	45
SECTION TWO: How to Future	63
5. Lay the Groundwork	65
6. Choosing Your Futurists	77
7. Mapping Your World	101
8. The Night Before Futuring	111
9. The Future is Now	119
10. Challenges for the Facilitator	133
11. Making Sense of the Future	143
12. Keeping the Future Present	151
In Closing	157
About the Authors	161

SECTION ONE: THE WHAT AND WHY OF FUTURING

INTRODUCTION

"Imagination is more important than knowledge. For knowledge is limited, whereas imagination embraces the entire world, stimulating progress, giving birth to evolution." – Albert Einstein

"Hindsight is always 20/20." – Billy Wilder

The future is uncertain, but the science of predictability is the science of the future" - Ian Stewart, mathematician and writer

Futuring is tough - but what makes it tough also makes it invaluable, because it trains our adult brains to freely imagine again, as most of us have not since childhood. Not to set a goal, not to transact, not to check off a task, not to listen, not to collaborate - not to do any of those things that we do on a daily basis so we can show up at our day jobs and run our companies. Transactional thinking promises that if I show up as an adult, with all the requisite skills and knowledge for leadership, I move up the ladder. If I'm a newly-minted CEO at Company A, I'm already looking forward to my jump to Company B in two years, and I live or die by quarterly earnings reports, so it behooves me to stay grounded in short-term thinking. But that's not where innovation lives – in fact, it's where it goes to die. And if you're a leader in any industry, short-term thinking will eventually leave you rearranging the deck chairs on the Titanic.

If you're in pharma, you're planning ahead ten or twenty years with every commitment you make to a new drug or research and development investment. You're spending billions on a long shot – a bet that the future will recognize the value of what you've created, and reward you for it. But how much are you spending to shape that future – to create the desirable future that will buy the goods you're selling? Will that future look like today – and are you willing to bet everything on the assumption that it will? Will the future be ready for the new product you've designed when it rolls out fifteen years from now?

Most businesses approach the future via some variation on the strategic planning model, in which we define and describe the now, analyze our strengths and opportunities, then extrapolate on that data to create short-term predictions and strategies on which we can all agree. Some would suggest there is even lifecycle planning that looks out on the horizon five, ten or fifteen years out. It looks at the continued linearity of the present day, but is such an extrapolation really the best view of the future? And if it is the future, is it the one that is desired for our research, our product and our planet? As noted above, pharma requires a longer view, because the industry's timeline makes it uniquely susceptible to Black Swan types of events; icebergs that lurk unseen and unanticipated beyond strategic planning's short-sighted outlook. And you only have to hit one of those to go down.

Unlike strategic planning, Futuring isn't done by looking forward; it's done by using your imagination to put yourself into a future, then looking back to see how you got there – a kind of creative hindsight that gifts you with 20/20 vision. Futuring takes you to a naked space; a place where the attachments, loyalties, realities of where we live today, fall away – and you are free to speak in a way that conventions or beliefs or loyalties prevent you from doing in the world of now. Yes, planning matters and there will always be a place for it in a well-run enterprise. Futuring isn't intended to replace planning; it's intended to complement it, and to give you the opportunity to shape the future, rather than merely react to it as it arrives.

Fortune 500 companies, especially those in the tech and automotive sector, are jumping on the Futuring bandwagon because they don't want to find themselves where the Big Three car companies were in the late '70s, and because they live in an industry that faces disruptive change on many fronts. Ford has a CFO – Chief Futuring Officer – on their payroll, because they recognize that for them, the future is all about innovation, whether that's self-driving cars or electric vehicles; it's not about upgrading the quality of leather that they use on their seats or how good the GPS system is, but what the next big jump will be.

Can those of us in healthcare really afford to think smaller than Ford? We would argue that our responsibility to the future is greater than that. As Beth Comstock, former Vice Chair of GE said in an interview with *Forbes*, "Often people say, "Can we just get through this bit of change before we start the next?" and you can't. You don't have the luxury to say, 'We'll get to this later.'"

Why isn't Futuring routinely taught in business school, as dependably as other tools like strategic planning are? Clearly, it needs to be, but in our observation B-school curricula predictably lag behind real-world changes in the way things are done. Futuring is still widely misunderstood and often dismissed as "touchy/feely" by those who don't appreciate its potential to unshackle our minds from the tyranny of the now. Yet, icebergs are out there; and if we can't make the imaginative leaps required to anticipate and avoid their impact, we're sunk, deck chairs and all.

ONE

WHY FUTURE?

"In 2004, Ford Motor Company's resident futurist, Sheryl Connelly, led a team that imagined what would happen if an economic shock and a rapid increase in the price of gasoline led to a crash in automotive sales. With the 2008 economic crash and subsequent bailout of the U.S. auto industry, it seemed as if their scenario had come true.

But did Ms. Connelly and her team really predict the future?"
– Christopher Mims, <u>Thinking Like a Futurist to be Prepared For the Totally Unexpected</u>, The Wall Street Journal, December 30, 2016

THE SHORT ANSWER to the question posed above is an emphatic "no": Nobody can predict the future, not even the unquestionably brilliant Ms. Connelly. And none of the tools that business typically uses to prepare for the future – forecasting and strategic planning, for instance – can lift that veil, either. If prediction is your game, you might as well rely on the Magic 8 Ball. It's cheaper, and vague enough in its answers to satisfy anybody.

But Futuring can do something better; it can help you to anticipate and explore many possible futures, while preparing you to identify the markers of change – the signposts – that pop up along the way, so that you can pivot and adjust your aims and strategies accordingly as the actual future unfolds. Monitoring those signposts is not just a matter of watching and waiting but rather using the outcomes from the Futuring session to identify the key areas to proactively track. Forward-looking organizations such as Ford, IBM, the Department of Defense, Shell Oil, Rockwell, Walmart, Mars and Nike strive to shape their futures via major investments in Futuring, because it keeps them nimble, vital, and ahead of their rivals.

AT SIMPSON HEALTHCARE we work with the leading pharmaceutical, biotechnology, patient advocacy leaders, medical diagnostic and device companies, and health technology, providing a wide range of consulting and marketing services in support of products and brands that have the potential to make the world a better place for people. Our corporate "why" is simple: we wake up every day determined to create better health in the world. And while our entrepreneurial founders are always looking toward the horizon, our core business keeps us busy, and growing like kudzu.

Our company's initial foray into Futuring was inspired by a client's problem. This global pharmaceutical giant was facing a challenge: A portfolio of medications they were developing wouldn't be ready to take to market for ten to fifteen years. But what would the healthcare landscape look like by then, and especially the landscape around the disease these medications treated? How would new technology be deployed in this landscape? Where would the patients be? Who might want those medications, and how would they be paid for? How might they be administered, and by whom? Obviously, these were pressing questions – and a lot of money was riding on the insights that could be derived around the potential future for these issues. Did we have a process in place that would help them to strategize now for what might be coming that far down the road?

We did what we usually do when handed a client's dilemma – we got into a room together to brainstorm it. It was Sheryl who first brought up the idea of Futuring; she'd done it before with another pharmaceutical company, and was confident of its value, especially in a scenario like this one.

The more we researched and discussed it, the better it sounded. Futuring after all wasn't new; leading thinkers and the military had been successfully using versions of Futuring since the 40s, and Alvin Toffler further explored the notion with his groundbreaking book, *Future Shock*, published in 1970. With refinements along the way, Futuring has been used to game everything from the outcome of a global thermonuclear conflict, to what kind of car design would have the most powerful appeal to Millennials. It was already being applied to healthcare, an increasingly unstable environment that was becoming harder and harder to predict. For example, there have been significant efforts to address health inequity over the past ten years via Futuring[1]. The approach to Futuring heretofore had been comprehensive but lengthy, and we felt there was an opportunity to refine a process to be more suitable to our current day environment, in which time is the ultimate luxury and budgets are squeezed to the max. Clearly, Futuring was a valuable skill – but it needed to be adapted and streamlined if it was to serve our clients' planning processes.

It seemed like a natural fit: We knew the pharma world, the players, the landscape, and how things work (or don't) currently. We had ideas around how to make the Futuring process less academic and more compact than previous models we'd seen; all the creative disruptiveness, but with less actual disruption to the company going through the process, given that very few companies have the resources that Ford or IBM does and aren't ready to have full-time Futurists on their payrolls. A pared-down, speed version – "with all of the flavor and none of the fat" - could work anywhere, and might be the logjam breaker our client needed at this critical decision point.

We took that idea and framework back to the pharma client, who gave our enthusiastic pitch a qualified "no"; while they liked us and were curious to know more about what we were offering, it was a little too edgy for them; "But stay in touch – we're interested in what you're talking about."

Six months later, they called us back, because the agency they'd brought on to help was getting on with the bread and butter, but the company was now ready for our more experimental ideas. There was a sudden call for more innovation or (dare we say it?) disruption. Ha! The people in charge could see that ordinary strategic planning tools and processes didn't afford them the opportunity to collectively imagine the future they wanted. No existing methodology allowed any consideration of a future beyond the next year or two. The company management were ready to change things up, because they saw the need for bigger thinking, and that's what we were offering. The client was clear; "Try, and fail – but try. I'm happy with that." That was an empowering mandate for management, and an opportunity for us to begin our first process of disruption with a Pharma client.

We did some more in-house brainstorming and, through a combination of deep thinking and imagination, we came up with a process and system that was tailored for this client; not one that would push us into Wacky World, but one that would bring the best minds from across multiple disciplines to the table with the people involved in the initiative at the corporation, and get them to exercise their imaginations together to create plausible scenarios around the future – coming up with the "what ifs", identifying those events that could alter the landscape, and what the most productive, proactive responses to those events should be. And in our model, this could be accomplished in days, not weeks or months or quarters of the year.

Futuring with this company was a great success, spawning fresh ideas and collaborations across silos and beyond, and led us to more Futuring with other clients in the healthcare space. The company looked specifically at the future in the US as a start, then we grew even bolder and flew across the pond to lead a Futuring collaborative with our global colleagues at the same company. What started as a way to help one client with one specific problem has grown to be a core part of what we do – and we're improving on our original model with every iteration.

WHY DOES this matter to us – and why should you be on board with Futuring? We'd suggest it's because health and healthcare are areas in which Futuring can literally be a matter of life and death. We can't afford to get it wrong, or to leave the future to chance. In general, the broader your scope, the further out you can look in your Futuring. For healthcare as a whole it makes sense to look 20 to 50 years out, given the large number of forces and factors that impact healthcare, and the diverse players. Context matters, and the bigger the problem, the more of it you need for the best shot at true disruption. A major challenge in the pharma world is the years-long developmental time line for a new drug or therapy, especially in an often-crowded and uncertain marketplace. Maybe you've got some potential products in your portfolio that won't see the market for another fifteen years; or you're producing something for which you need to identify a new market. Perhaps when you enter that crowded market you need a way to differentiate your product and your company. How will the delivery of medicines and healthcare look in 2030 or 2040, and how will your product fit into this future landscape? What can you do to position it early enough, before the future is so far along that it cannot be reframed? How can you be quicker to spot the indicators of change on the horizon that will impact your product, and respond to them faster? How can you shape what's coming, rather than be stuck reacting to it once it's here?

Futuring gives you the ability to proactively identify and track the indicators of change – those signposts we mentioned earlier – and thus to navigate change better than your competition. Thinking about the future in this way fundamentally changes the way you think about the decisions you're making today. Futuring provides a novel context that allows you to make a smarter decision *right now*. In this book, we want to tell you our story of Futuring so that you will be equipped to harness the power of Futuring in your own organization, and be ready to start thinking and acting differently.

"In an era when there's so much data coming at you and so much acceleration of information, it's hard to step back, pause, and have clarity on the future because the future is an hour from now, and whatever happened three minutes ago is already old news." - Kelly

---

How is what we're doing different from other Futuring? We'll dig into this in depth in the coming pages, but here's the short version: Very often Futuring is broad and, by design, divergent in its focus. Drilling down to specific, meaningful, actionable steps that will shape your market and your space going forward can take a while. In contrast, our process gets very granular quickly, identifying specific drivers shaping the market so that you can actively look for and spot them if and when they show up.

Futuring's outcomes and insights can be rendered moot, however, if nobody is tasked with occasionally hitting "refresh" and taking stock of where you are vis a vis the future you've envisioned and the indicators or trends you've identified. To address this, we created the Simpson Futuring Model™ to make the routine of regularly surveying the evolving landscape through the lens of your Futuring insights part of your culture going forward. This has created a continuing return on investment for our clients, and made the process continuously relevant; if you don't commission someone to build on the world that you've created, to make things happen and to be disruptive, your Futuring goes nowhere.

In Section One, we'll talk about the what and why of Futuring; in Section Two we get down to nuts and bolts, using as examples two

Futurings we did with clients in the pharmaceutical world. While their questions and issues were quite different, their overarching problem - how do we shape a future in which health behaviors among all stakeholders improve the receptivity to our product in a competitive market? – was the same, and is one with which all companies in that space are familiar.

Pharma Alpha is an international biopharmaceutical company, one of the world's largest. They were planning the debut a new group of treatments for type 2 diabetes they'd be introducing internationally in about fifteen years. They were very aware that unmet medical need alone is not sufficient to compel stakeholders to embrace a new treatment entering a field that is already crowded -so what would compel them? The delivery system for this novel treatment worldwide may not be as robust as it needs to be, and will likely change – but how? They recognized that there are multiple barriers to the successful uptake of any new medicine; how could they understand the issues at play better, so they could address and overcome those barriers and increase the odds that their product will reach the right patients in a timely and affordable way when the products reach the market?

Pharma Beta is another well-known drug company, smaller than Alpha, with a number of legacy drugs in its portfolio. They're preparing to introduce a drug that treats a very rare condition – one afflicting only about three people per million. What will be the factors that will shape the landscape for this drug's viability in the next five to ten years? Will there be a place in the marketplace for new therapies as that space becomes more crowded? In the case of a rare disease, there are particular concerns to address, one being the under-diagnosis of the disease, and the difficulty of identifying the right patients for prompt treatment. There are fewer experts for rare disease than more common afflictions, and these can also be difficult to find. Pharma is focused on rare disease as we write, but this has not always been the case. How will the future for rare diseases develop, particularly if budgets in Big Pharma shrink in the years to come?

There are few areas of medicine where the skill and art of imagination can be more rewarding than in rare disease. It's worth noting here that our ability or willingness to let our imaginations run wild, so evident in childhood, tends to decrease in our teens and 20s. As we immerse ourselves in our grownup lives, our imaginative lives often get crowded out, and over time, we can lose the skill completely.

As we go through the steps of Futuring in Section Two, we'll get down to the particulars using the steps of these companies' Futuring endeavors as illustrative examples. While we won't be disclosing the specifics around their products, or using the real names of the participants or companies, you'll be able to get a clear idea of how it looks in action.

The best part about Futuring as we do it? Honestly, it's that nearly anyone who's open to thinking differently can do it, provided they have the mandate, the resources, the desire to learn the skill of Futuring, and the support of top management – to pull Futuring into your culture. In conceptualizing this book, we have been very deliberate in taking our model apart, explaining the moving parts, and putting it all together so that anyone can drive it once they understand what makes it go.

By the time you've finished it, you'll be ready to grab the wheel and begin Futuring in your organization.

KEY POINTS FOR CHAPTER ONE:

1. While Futuring can't predict the future, it can help you to explore and strategize for what might happen.
2. A major challenge in the pharma world is the years-long developmental time line for a new drug or therapy. Futuring prepares you to identify the markers of change – the signposts – so that you can pivot and adjust your aims and strategies accordingly as the actual future unfolds.

3. Futuring leads to insights and innovation.
4. Futuring is a skill that can be learned.
5. Our model of Speed Futuring can be done in days, rather than weeks.

---

1. link https://altfutures.org/projects/health-equity/

TWO
THE PAST AND PRESENT OF FUTURING

(IT'S A MENAGERIE OUT THERE!)

"*Forecasts are not always wrong; more often than not, they can be reasonably accurate. And that is what makes them so dangerous. They are usually constructed on the assumption that tomorrow's world will be much like today's. They often work because the world does not always change. But sooner or later forecasts will fail when they are needed most: in anticipating major shifts in the business environment that make whole strategies obsolete.*" - Pierre Wack, Uncharted Waters Ahead, HBR, Sept. 1985

"*This is how the present must be considered whenever we try to think about it as the past: It must be analyzed through the values of a future that's unwritten. Before we can argue that something we currently appreciate deserves inclusion in the world of tomorrow, we must build that future world within our mind. This is not easy (even with drugs). But it's not even the hardest part. The hardest part is accepting that we're building something with parts that don't yet exist.*" -Chuck Klosterman, But What If We're Wrong?: Thinking About the Present As If It Were the Past

. . .

"WHAT NEXT?" is a question we humans struggle - and fail - to reliably answer, despite our best efforts. The ability to predict, foresee, and influence the future, and the powers such a gift would give us have been the inspiration for comic books, classic literature, and a host of B movies – but the reality is, we're no closer to building a time machine than Jules Verne was. Failing that, our next-best option for engaging proactively with uncertainty is Futuring.

What we now call scenario planning - the basis of Futuring - wasn't an organized, reproducible discipline in the private realm until the late 1940s, when United States defense analyst and physicist Herman Kahn was brought aboard at the Rand Corporation to "think about the unthinkable"; specifically, to Future the possible outcomes of a nuclear conflict between the United States and Russia. Kahn coupled the day's most forward-thinking assessment technologies - operational research, computer science, systems analysis, and game theory - with his own prodigious intellect (it was said he had the highest IQ ever measured) and unconventional way of thinking.

What were his conclusions? The first was that nuclear war was certainly possible; the second (and far more controversial) conclusion was that it was winnable, although he believed the US could alternatively maintain peace through deterrence and by maintaining its second-strike capability. While acknowledging that the outcome of such a war would be devastating, he was able to demonstrate through scenario planning that it was in fact a survivable event for humanity, contrary to the Doomsday scenarios that most had envisioned around such an event. It was a game changer and his work has continued to inform Defense Department strategy for many years.

SHELL OIL FACED a similar dilemma in the 1960's. Planning and executing large-scale infrastructure projects meant making educated guesses about what the business of oil would look like in the future – but an in-house study suggested that the level of expansion to which they and others in the space had become accustomed could not continue indefinitely, that changes in supply, demand, and market were inevitable, and could challenge not only their dominance but their existence down the road.

That sobering realization led to Shell's exploring new ways to look ahead. In 1965, the head of economics and planning, Jimmy Davidson, asked Ted Newland, who had been with the company for many years, to start what they called Long Term Studies at Shell's headquarters in London. Newland's remit? To "think about the future". This preliminary venture into so-called scenarios led to the development and distribution of the groundbreaking Year 2000 report as well as the development of alternative futures with colleague Henk Alkema. Oil executive Pierre Wack of Royal Dutch Shell's London headquarters was brought in to secure the link to senior executives, and he used plausible stories to capture his audience.

With Newland, Wack defined scenario planning at Shell and, between them, they led the company through a turbulent decade that included two major oil crises, helping the company weather pricing and supply uncertainties that arose during those years. Together, they created and gamed out a series of alternative scenarios, which they presented to Shell executives to consider. Their emphasis in creating these scenarios was unthreatening plausibility, rather than normativity or probability. Unless there was some overwhelming logical reason why a scenario couldn't happen, it was on the table for consideration. Together they spun a scenario of political turmoil, an energy gap, and the potential for an energy crisis back in 1973, well before anyone else in the petroleum industry was considering such events. Their success led to Wack's being dubbed the "other" father of Futuring. Later, Peter Schwartz, who ran the scenario teams for Shell, took the process to the strategic consulting group, the Global Business Network, where Schwartz became known in the business world for his commitment and insight into what he called "the long view".

What made their Futuring so valuable? Wack and Newland were wary of what they called the "business as usual" attitude toward the future which had informed the company's planning, with its underlying assumption that things would generally proceed as they had before, seeing this as a sort of bias based solely on optimism. In their excellent analysis of Shell's continuing forays into Futuring as a tool for planning, Futurists Angela Wilkinson and Roland Kupers explained,

"*Shell scenarios are intended to set the stage for a future world in which readers imagine themselves as actors and are invited to pay attention to deeply held assumptions about how that world works. What happens at a scenario's horizon date is not as important as the storyline's clarity of logic and how it helps open the mind to new dynamics. Plausible stories encourage judgment, not just attention to data and other information. By acknowledging that subjective judgment and intuition are an integral part of the leadership process, scenarios create a safe space in which to acknowledge uncertainty. An intuitive understanding of the world precedes and frames the analytical understanding that follows. Intuition is the essence of entrepreneurial value creation, and it can be stifled by a paralysis of analysis. Plausibility can be strengthened by how relevant and memorable the scenario is, as well as by a logical story line.*" [1]

Thus, when the first oil crisis hit in 1973 – the result of the Arab members of OPEC declaring an oil embargo against the US in retaliation for US support of Israeli military in the Yom Kippur War – Shell was able to see it coming and to deal with the fallout expeditiously. Shell's Futurists had already gamed out a scenario that looked a lot like that which precipitated it, two years previously; a plausible future in which the oil-producing nations would decide to cut production rather than continue to raise it as they had in the past, causing prices to spike under the pressure the resultant shortages created. When it played out very much as they'd suggested it might, they were hailed as forecasters, but resisted that label, insisting rather that they were "personal trainers"; in other words, there to strengthen the company's ability to engage in creative, "what if...?" thinking that many if not most people find difficult to adopt – but which is necessary to successful Futuring. Shell executives learned to listen - and Futuring still holds a key place in the company's strategy and planning today.

FUTURING HAS HAD a powerful impact on the direction taken by other legacy corporations at the crossroads, too, outside of the oil industry. Sheryl Connelly, Global Consumer Trends and Futuring Manager at Ford Motor Company and a Futurist there since 2004, uses research and Futuring to predict consumer trends and potential hazards. In 2004, she and her team posed a daunting question: What would happen if a gasoline price spike resulted in a sudden fall of auto sales for Ford? The possibility of that happening led Ford to look at ways to survive a crash of the magnitude she suggested could come about – and when an economic crash did hit in 2008, Ford was the only one among the Big Three auto makers that didn't require a bailout. In the first decade of the new millennium, Connelly's research revealed the likelihood that aging baby boomers were going to feel less confident in their driving, thanks to slowing reflexes and poorer eyesight. That insight pointed a new direction for the company, into the development of features meant to enhance safety and driver confidence, like blind spot alert and automated parking assistance. Her yearly breakdown of the research she and her staff do and the indicators she gleans from it continue to play an important role in the company's long-term strategizing.

As was the case with Shell, Ford is the corporate equivalent of an ocean liner, and you don't turn an ocean liner at a moment's notice. The infrastructure required to manufacture cars takes years to design and to build – and wrong choices can mean many lean years of lost opportunity. The US auto industry's failure to respond to pressure from the Japanese auto manufacturers in the areas of production quality, reliability and smaller car size back in the early 80's nearly caused its collapse, and that shift in consumer demands was a development that V-8 obsessed Detroit never saw coming until it was nearly too late. But what if they had? Like everyone but Shell in the oil industry, the major automakers were lulled into a false sense of security by "business as usual" thinking.

BUSINESS HAS COME up with an array of practical tools to help executives charged with planning to forecast, strategically plan for, and be nimbler in adapting to the future. But none of these offers ways to actually change that future – only to cope with what it's likely to dish out. And the concept of what's called a Black Swan event's ability to turn the cart over entirely isn't accounted for in these models of prediction and forecasting.

The theory of Black Swan events was introduced by Nicholas Taleb in his 2001 book, *Fooled by Randomness: The Hidden Role of Chance in the Markets and In Life*[2], to explain major shifts in financial markets that were unpredicted. He later expanded on the topic in his book, *The Black Swan: The Impact of the Highly Improbable*[3], and extended the concept to areas outside of finance. For Taleb, in order for an event to qualify as a Black Swan, it must be unexpected, have a high impact, and rationalized after the fact -thus making it seem predictable (at least retrospectively). Examples include the Internet, smart phones, and the 9/11 attacks on the World Trade Center. Some of these happen suddenly, while others are in progress for years before appearing as an unexpected phenomenon. For all Black Swans, predicting them is not the goal, but remaining resilient in the face of them is. So, while Futuring may not always allow you to predict a Black Swan, it does prepare you to deal with it more expeditiously should one show up.

Not to make this all about animals, but we would be remiss not to mention two others who have roles to play; the Red Herring and the Elephant in the Room, both mischievous creatures that can interfere with our view of both the present and the future. While we are typically underprepared for the Black Swan, we are over-prepared for the Red Herring and fastidiously avoidant of the Elephant in the Room.

Readers of mysteries are familiar with the notion of the Red Herring, which presents itself as a useful clue, but is actually misleading and false and intended to guide the reader to forming incorrect assumptions about the crime. The Red Herring lures us in with its seductive ideas, convincing us we are onto something, only to fizzle out after commanding time and resources that could have been directed to more fruitful ventures.

A classic example of a Red Herring is a scientific revelation that announces, for example, "Eating pork extends the lifespan". A study has shown that people who eat pork appear to live longer than those who do not. "Show me the pig!", we think. However, such studies usually conflate correlation and causation, and on closer inspection, and perhaps after a few bestsellers on the health benefits of pork chops and barbecue, it can be noted that the finding was a mere correlation, with no actual evidence of causation. While this may seem a trivial example, think of the millions of dollars spent trying to find medicines to reduce amyloid deposition in the brains of Alzheimer patients. It is still not clear whether the amyloid is cause or effect of the disease, and targeting the protein has had little true effect on the disease to date. This type of Red Herring can be costly, and divert resources from other theories that may yield a better outcome for the patient.

One way to be alert to (and avoid swallowing) potential Red Herrings is to monitor changes over time, using the outcomes of Futuring as our guide. As soon as a hot trend begins to go cold, we can reasonably suspect a Red Herring is in play, and adjust our attention accordingly. Again, we identify these as a signpost of the future in the making. It is certainly directional and should offer a reason for pause, thinking and integration of these signposts into both the "long view" and the short-term tools we use more annually. We may glom onto the trend for a moment in time, but it is important to let it go when the time is right. This can be easier said than done, and not letting go is a reason that some researchers get stuck into dead-end research paths for most of their careers: After investing years of their lives in a theory, it can be simply too hard to just move on.

The Elephant in the Room (or the Dead Moose on the Table for British readers) is another tricky character that we don't want to talk about, even though we're all uncomfortably aware of its presence in the room. Not acknowledging the elephant can undermine the most carefully thought-out and agreed-upon plans. Futuring can help us deal more productively with this guy, too. By providing a safe place for imagination and even conflict, Futuring gives us the opportunity to call out the Elephant in the Room without offense or risk. We avoid political harm in a corporation because, while we all may be thinking it, there is often no allowance to bring that thought forward. Futuring offers a setting in which to identify these elephants in a safe, non-political package.

Our discussion on animals would be incomplete if we didn't also mention the Gray Rhino at this point. According to Michele Wucker[4] who wrote the book about it, a "gray rhino" is a *"highly probable, high impact yet neglected threat: kin to both the elephant in the room and the improbable and unforeseeable Black Swan. Gray rhinos are not random surprises, but occur after a series of warnings and visible evidence."* She uses as examples, the bursting of the housing bubble in 2008, the aftermath of Hurricane Katrina, and the new digital technologies that disrupted the world of media. She also includes the fall of the Soviet Union. These events should have been predictable but the signposts leading up to them were ignored so they seemed more like black swans than gray rhinos (We'll be discussing these more extensively further on, but we thought it was good to introduce the animals early. It's a menagerie out there!).

And while she doesn't (strictly speaking) belong in the menagerie, let's not forget the unfortunate Cassandra of Greek mythology who, upon rejecting the amorous advances of Apollo, was cursed by that god to always tell the truth but never to be believed. Modern-day Cassandras would certainly include those who first spoke up about the oncoming catastrophe of climate change. Why Cassandras are so often dismissed and even mocked by most people is worthy of research in itself, but we can safely assume that it says more about us than it does about Cassandra.

FUTURING INFORMS a new hyperawareness of the environment at large, allowing you to see the significance in events you might not otherwise spot, and to act upon those events in a way that helps you shape what comes next. It allows you to pause for a moment and use the information coming your way to shape your future some ten to twenty years from now. Futuring enables you to bring together seemingly disparate elements and see them as part of the greater whole; to take the 30,000-mile view. But the real gift is that Futuring changes you. Once you learn the methods, tools, and skills to imagine a variety of "futures", it shifts everything about the way you view the world and your ability to affect it. It allows you to shift your mental model, because Futuring helps you to make change, consciously and by choice. It's not about predicting, but imagining, then doing things along the way to make that unfolding future align with what you want to have happen. It empowers you to actually shift its direction, not just ride its wake.

Futuring isn't unique; thousands of people Future. It's how we do it, and how we've adapted it to the current, time-compressed world of healthcare, that's new.

What are scenarios?

We know that facts alone do not move people to action, but experience certainly can. The scenarios allow us to make a potential situation more real by making the "facts" of the future more relatable.

Here is how we describe them:

- Scenarios are above all, stories. They are essentially "what ifs...?"

- They're stories of potential and plausible futures
- They are the products of imagination; an idea, and not set in stone
- They exist to provide frameworks for discussion that are based on human experience
- They encourage conversation that is *qualitatively* different than conversation in the absence of scenarios. They allow space for actively questioning assumptions

They inform:

- Immediate actions that may be needed
- Areas for deep-dive exploration
- Key areas that require ongoing monitoring

We should remember that the role of Futuring is not as a stand-alone concept, but rather a companion to planning and vision work. It is a missing piece that complements long-term planning and can further inform our annual plans. Futuring allows us to answer certain questions that planning and visioning can take for granted, such as where you really want to go, and what environment you will have to work through to get there.

How does our model of Futuring differ from others?

First, this iteration of Futuring is designed to answer specific challenges in the healthcare sphere. Second, it's devised to be done in a much shorter span of time – a kind of speed dating with the future, if you like – while producing meaningful, actionable results.

Our model recognizes that most companies just don't have the resources to future on the scale of Ford or Shell, so we've adapted our methodology to accomplish more with less. Our process is adaptable and nimble, and its scope is tailored to what the client needs; for some, more narrowly focused on the scientific future, while for others, taking a broader look at larger healthcare-level questions.

> *"What differentiates our model is that it's cost effective, and it's time effective for companies that need efficient solutions. It allows for a taste of the "dark" or "light" futures, rather than fully fleshing them out, and leaves you with ideas for new projects, allows you to build approval internally, provides strategic pillars that can guide your decision making and signposts you can actually track, sometimes resulting in a new internal decision making and/or working group."* – Sheryl

> *"Futuring allows us to apply a more relevant and predictive look at long term and life cycle planning. If we can see it and imagine it, we can shape it and prepare for it with leadership and presence."* – Kelly

TRADITIONAL FUTURING OFTEN REQUIRES MULTIPLE multi-day sessions – but just as nobody today has the patience to watch a video that's over three minutes long, the idea of spending more than a couple of days Futuring can be off-putting, especially with our overcrowded schedules. Our model follows a manageable and abbreviated format, taking just two days annually, with a follow-up meeting to discuss how to convert the findings to action plans and integrate them into components of corporate, clinical portfolio, and product long term planning, along with direction or assistance in creating an ongoing review and reset as events continue to unfold, as markets evolve and the signposts reveal themselves, allowing the client to adjust their strategies as the future's direction becomes more clear.

What does successful Futuring require?

First, it demands buy-in by people who are willing to consider doing something different in your organization, based on the recognition that if you aren't Futuring, you are not optimally positioned to anticipate your market and its evolution. In our experience, the culture of the companies that choose to incorporate Futuring into their planning toolbox are the ones focused on innovation, disruption and dynamic leadership. Ask yourself if your organization is built on these principles. If your answer is "yes," then Futuring should be part of your organization's planning process.

Futuring needs an internal champion high up in the organization who can help support and drive the shift needed internally to embrace this approach. Futuring requires organizational courage and if your potential Futurists simply lack that courage or the imagination to do it, the Futuring will not go anywhere; it can't. That is why it is important to think critically about who from within the company should attend the session.

It also requires a commitment to work to keep the future present in your thinking. Once you've been through a Futuring exercise, it should change the lens through which you view the present from now forward.

What can Futuring accomplish that the more conventional ways of looking ahead – strategic planning, forecasting, etc. – do not?

Futuring changes the conversation among core stakeholders and frees us up to go beyond the assumptions we hold today. The perspective generated by that change of viewpoint creates a different kind of conversation around making present-day decisions. At best this process helps us shape a "desired future"; at the least, it helps us avoid impact from an "undesirable" one. The overall aim is to catalyze disruptive transformation in the industry itself, whether is it healthcare, automotive, energy, and so forth.

How is this different from long-term planning?

They're yin and yang; unlike planning in which your point of view is today and you work forward, in Futuring you jump out into the future, then work back. Futuring should change the decisions you make today. If it does not, then it's of no use to you. The future is relevant now. Futuring and long-term planning are both necessary and complementary, and when used effectively provide an opportunity for an ongoing iterative process that allows for readjustment of today's plan based on new insights from continuing environmental monitoring. With some Futuring, it may be one and done: The outcomes may be integrated into business plans for the future, but the exercise is not repeated, and there is limited ongoing monitoring to track signposts that may indicate a shift in course is appropriate. For us, Futuring works best when it is integrated into business as usual, with the outcomes of Futuring integrated into your business plans for the future, coupled with a dedicated effort to track signposts and continue to reassess your direction and ultimate goals. To this end we recommend incorporating Futuring into your business planning at regular intervals; if you're in a fast-moving business, every year.

AS WAS the case with the global market for oil for Shell, the success of the products of pharmaceutical research, development and marketing depends on making the right choices for the future, today – without the benefit of a crystal ball. As it stands, pharma sees a need and moves to fill it; to create a vaccine, a cure, a medication for an existing disease or condition which they're betting will find a market down the road, based on what they know about today. But in a world as uncertain, shifting and volatile as ours, assuming that the future will look like "more of the same" isn't a viable strategy – and neither is forecasting. As Pierre Wack said,

"The better approach, I believe, is to accept uncertainty, try to understand it, and make it part of our reasoning. Uncertainty today is not just an occasional, temporary deviation from reasonable predictability; it is a basic structural feature of the business environment. The method used to think about and plan for the future must be made appropriate to a changed business environment."

SO - HOW DO we begin to embrace the unknown future, and to make it our ally, rather than the invisible enemy? That starts with making space for it to happen –in our busy work world, in our imaginations, and in our business practices today and tomorrow. The practice of Futuring in each organization should be one of intention and importance, driven by a sense of urgency. As a leader, you want to do it now, because leading without a sense for the desired future can prevent you from truly leading.

Key points for Chapter 2

1. Futuring is radically different from but complementary to strategic planning.
2. Futuring doesn't have to be expensive or lengthy; our blueprint is effective and efficient.
3. Futuring requires organizational courage, but the rewards are significant; It will require an internal champion as high up in the organization as you can find.
4. Futuring gives you a process to manage the unknown and the unknowable, to drive toward a future you desire, instead of reacting to one you don't.

5. Futuring should be a regular event that is intentionally incorporated into your annual and long-term planning.

---

1. Angela Wilkinson and Roland Kupers, "Living in the Futures; How Scenario Planning Changed Corporate Strategy", Harvard Business Review, May 2013
2. Taleb, Nassim Nicholas, 1960-. Fooled By Randomness : the Hidden Role of Chance in the Markets and in Life. New York: Texere, 2001.
3. Taleb, Nassim Nicholas, 1960-. The Black Swan : the Impact of the Highly Improbable. New York :Random House, 2007.
4. Wucker, Michele: The Grey Rhino: How to Recognize and Act on the Obvious Dangers We Ignore: 2016, St. Martin's Press, New York

THREE
CREATE THE PAUSE
MAKING TIME TO FUTURE

"The important task rarely must be done today, or even this week...but the urgent task calls for instant action...The momentary appeal of these tasks seems irresistible and important, and they devour our energy. But in the light of time's perspective, their deceptive prominence fades; with a sense of loss we recall the vital tasks we pushed aside. We realize we've become slaves to the tyranny of the urgent." - Charles Hummel, The Tyranny of the Urgent

"Once you start daydreaming and allow your mind to really wander you start thinking a little bit beyond the conscious and a little bit into the subconscious which allows... different connections to take place." – Dr. Sandi Mann

WHAT KEEPS US FROM FUTURING?

The first impediment for most of us is purely practical: Given the pace the world keeps, it's not surprising that the idea of taking additional time to focus on the future too is overwhelming for many companies and individuals. Our everyday work lives are solidly moored to the present, and work's demands seem positively Sisyphean as we roll that same boulder up the same hill every day.

Futuring is not familiar to many of us. If we're coming to this from the business side and B-School, Futuring was unlikely to have been part of our formal education. While strategic planning skills, including scenario planning, are front and center of any business school education, the fundamental skill of Futuring is not generally taught in business school so is not top of mind for most company executives or the consultants they bring aboard to help them with their strategic thinking. Yet, without the skill of imagination, necessary to fan out the multiple possibilities before us, we're most likely going to base our visions of what the future holds on what we've already seen and experienced. It's hard to be a visionary if you're in a culture that doesn't support or respect Futuring; it requires sticking your neck out – and the skill of imagining is one that many of us leave behind in childhood, assuming we were given the opportunity to exercise and develop it even then. Were you taught how to imagine? Does society give us permission to imagine, or is imagination for the unfocused and unrealistic dreamers of society?

Our attention span's bandwidth is fully engaged 24/7 thanks to omnipresent phones, social media, the internet of everything, the avalanche of emails, and what author Charles Hummel called "the tyranny of the urgent". Yes, we've got more access to the world's accumulated knowledge than any previous generation could boast – along with a lot of misinformation and an endless stream of cute puppy videos. We need never be bored. But the cost of this Faustian bargain may be our ability to free our minds to imagine. In her excellent TEDtalk, *How Boredom Helps You Do Your Best Thinking*, Manoush Zomorodi talks about the value of letting your mind roam without restriction or interruptions – what many of us would classify as boredom. In this state, as when we're performing a mechanical, repetitive household chore that doesn't require our concentration, she explains, our *"body goes on autopilot. This is when we connect disparate ideas, and when we solve some of our most nagging problems. And this is when we do what's called autobiographical planning. We look back at our lives, we take note of the big moments, we create a personal narrative, and then we set goals and we figure what the steps are we need to take to reach them."*

Yet the majority of us give very little time to this kind of free-range daydreaming, much less for thinking in any depth about the future. Will the future be better or the same? Most of us don't see it as being worse – but it does seem remote and out of our hands. Can we affect what the future becomes? Many of us may pride ourselves on how little down-time we need. But what if we could use that down-time more effectively? Allowing ourselves to pause can refresh, revitalize and stimulate our imagination in unexpected ways. Why not use the pause button in our business lives, to create space for imagination in the form of Futuring? When we think of this this way, it becomes more a question of why not, than a question of why.

Added to the practical obstacles, talking about the future at work can feel unsafe, as though we're trying to rock the boat. Those of us who work in a corporate culture know from experience that despite high-flown vision and mission statements, leadership may or may not actually support thinking differently.

But Futuring provides an environment in which people can safely disagree with each other or challenge the commonly accepted wisdom that informs the status quo of today and tomorrow. In planning, disagreement is a challenge; in Futuring, disagreement is an asset. Disagreement, passion and differences are necessary to the recipe of Futuring. In an environment of Futuring, consensus and conflict dance, until they settle or they don't. As Shell's Ted Newland put it,

"In hindsight, the greatest value of scenarios is that they created a culture where you could ask anyone a question, and the answer would need to be contextual. Answering, "Because I'm the boss" or "Because the business case is positive" was out of bounds."

We may not agree about what the landscape will look like in our particular areas of interest ten or twenty years down the line, but certainly we know it won't look the same as it does today. While Futuring does not provide a tangible deliverable with a key performance indicator (KPI) we can report to Wall Street next quarter, it does create readiness and attention to our viability, and impacts our ability to thrive and our market readiness. It can mean the difference between finding ourselves in the winner's circle, or out of the race.

Stifled by silos

Another impediment to Futuring in a corporate setting is the way in which corporations are typically structured; in silos. When we're working in corporations, we tend not to look over the top of our own particular silo. I have my objectives; you have yours. I have my role, you have yours. I have my deliverables, you have yours. I have my KPI, you have yours. While our goals may intersect at some point down the road, we're each focused on meeting our own objectives, and changing the future is beyond our remit. My day job is not to change the future; my day job is to grow the market, sell the drug, create a patient campaign; whatever it is. Unless I'm a designated Futurist within the company, the future is someone else's job. Even so, the human factor is alive in each of us, but dormant, waiting to wake up and Future. Some would call this our "child self" who can step back and bring forth the skill of imagination, but with the wisdom of an adult.

> *"Healthcare is largely focused on short-term objectives, and the people in it are incentivized, promoted, and recognized by management for executing against these things which have nothing to do with the long term in shaping the future. What's unique about this process is that it forces them to think longer term, beyond those day to day objectives, and incentivizes them to do things relevant to shaping the future."* - Erin

The problem with living in silos is that they block our view – and keep us doing the same things in the same ways, plugging along a day at a time. Every silo has its own politics, its leaders and laggards, and its own subculture within the larger culture of the organization. Those who labor in them may not be thinking in terms of the future, because frankly they're not sure where they'll be when it gets here. Given the turnover we see across the divisions in healthcare companies, they're not wrong in thinking, "I might not care what the company looks like in ten years, because I'll have moved on. We only spend a couple of years in each role and I don't get bonuses for what the future might be; I get paid for what I do in the here and now."

BUT THE FUTURE belongs to those with the imagination to envision it and consider its possibilities. Look at the advances made in the last half century that have changed the world so completely – and how few of us saw them coming, or the value in them when they first arrived. Steve Wozniak and Steve Jobs grasped the potential for putting a computer in every home back in 1975, an idea that seemed unworkable and impractical to Wozniak's employer, Hewlett Packard, who turned down their design for the Apple I five different times. The ubiquitous cell phone – now a tiny computer in its own right – was just a clunky prototype in 1973, and the notion that dinner tables around the world would be populated by families checking their Instagram and FaceBook accounts would surely have been dismissed as nonsense. Today, lasers are used in almost every conceivable setting, from manufacturing to surgery – but when they were invented in 1975, nobody really knew what they might be good for. Amidst wild speculation about their usefulness (or lack of it) Pierre Aigran (then the Secretary of State for Research and member of the Academy of Sciences) said,

"We are used to having a problem and looking for a solution. In the case of the laser, we already have the solution, we just have to find the problem."

And then there are the discoveries that seemed too important not to change the world, but expectations from the initial hype are vastly different from reality where technical challenges, ethical hurdles and simply a lack of scientific understanding can mean many years between a discovery and true human impact. Mapping the human genome was seen as the dawn of a revolution that would rapidly lead to the creation of a new class of "designer" medicines. The idea was irresistible to the media and the public at large, so expectations were high - but also highly unrealistic. In many ways, this was a bit of a Red Herring, not with regard to the eventual outcome but with respect to the timing. It has taken many years for the structure of the genome to yield practical insights that allowed for the development of personalized medicines. One reason for the slow progress was the failure of the media and those creating the hype to consider everything else that has to be in place for the genetics of a disorder to be translated to the actual practice of medicine. While the genes were now in plain sight, understanding the interactions between them, the factors that influenced their expression through particular proteins, and the contribution to the complexities of health and disease were still far into the future. Only now, as we write, has personalized medicine really begun to take off in areas beyond cancer, where it made its mark first.

The tools and techniques for analyzing genes have brought tremendous insights to scientific research, genealogy and law enforcement, but for medicine, we are just getting started. We have medicines that are targeted to specific tumors for example, and we can use genetic analysis to tell us whether we will respond to certain drugs, or will experience particular side effects in some cases. Our knowledge and understanding of genetics have increased exponentially since the mapping of the genome, but we have struggled mightily to apply our findings to the bedside. The biotech and pharma worlds are working closely with physicians and scientists to turn this knowledge into new medicines but there are many problems yet to solve and the field is certainly ripe for Futuring.

Other disciplines are always needed for the discussion, including ethicists, digital health experts, data security professionals, healthcare payers - and the list goes on. We'll talk more about this a little later, when we discuss how we choose our Futurists. As we will see, part of the process in Futuring is identifying the full breadth of stakeholders and making sure they are represented in the room when we future. One key growing challenge in our ever-connected world is how we break down the silos and work across disciplines to bring the best health solutions to patients. Again, Futuring can help us see possibilities that would not be apparent by looking around us today, or by talking to the same old people about the same old problems. We need to reframe the conversation and freshen up our view of who our future stakeholders are likely to be.

What can Futuring help us solve?

We don't need to look further than the challenges already in front of us, or looming on the horizon, to see why those of us in healthcare need to lead through Futuring. How can we as patients, or potential patients, interact more efficiently with the healthcare system? How, for instance, do you make people aware of the new drugs or new ways to understand disease risk or new diagnostic platforms in a fresh way that will inform them and get them to actually ask their doctors about them?

We've been able to advertise direct to consumers (DTC) for about 20 years as of this writing – but the style and messaging of today's drug infomercials hasn't changed substantively in all that time, and it's still not doing the job it's supposed to do. Typically, these ads feature a couple of minutes of "Here's the drug, and what it treats" followed by the required safety language for a minute and a half, ending with a tagline, some flowery music, and a soft-focus shot of an attractive older couple holding hands on a park bench or walking on the beach –a formula that's pretty much unchanged since it debuted twenty years ago. It can actually be worse when an agency gets a little too creative – our favorite example being a billboard campaign that featured just the name of the drug, with the tag line, "Ask your healthcare provider". You have to wonder how many people got curious and did "ask their healthcare provider" - only to find out it was a drug meant to treat substance abuse! The statin drug Lipitor did it better (and enjoyed huge success) with their memorable tagline, "What's your number?", but that was a bright spot in a pretty flat DTC landscape, and a decade ago to boot. Why is it that with all the money and creative minds trying to find a way to make ads that do what they're supposed to do, we're still basically where we started?

HERE'S another challenge that needs to be met: What can be done about the appalling rate of maternal deaths in childbirth in the United States, where more women die of pregnancy-related complications than in any other developed country? According to statistics from the CDC, and despite our spending more on healthcare than any other country in the world, as many as 900 women died in childbirth in the US in 2016 – and the CDC states that 60% of those deaths were preventable. How could better prenatal care improve that abysmal record, and how can we reach the women who aren't getting care at all? Again, it's an issue that some of the best minds are wrestling with, but without success.

Regarding healthcare in general, the US spends more per capita than any other country, but has some of the worst health outcomes.[1] Despite its status as one of the world's most developed and powerful countries, the US is generally ranked the worst on measures of success, including access, administration, health equity, and health outcome domains. The countries that ranked the highest overall were the UK, Australia and the Netherlands. Clearly, the health system in the US appears to be broken. It is worth noting that in every Futuring session we have conducted, healthcare as a right and subsequently universal access to it is central to the vision of the desired future. In reality, even the humble gains in health coverage made by the Affordable Care Act are under constant threat from political wrangling. Even the most innovative products to come out of pharma in the next decade or more will struggle to find success if the situation does not improve. Modern medicines of the 2020s will be challenged by the payer landscape– how will they be supported and paid for? Will someone figure out how to fix our kidneys or grow new ones, and wipe out the $114 billion paid by the U.S. government each year to treat chronic kidney disease and end-stage renal disease? Any assessment of the path to market for any product or device will certainly be incomplete unless Futuring is conducted to understand the potential shifts in the broader healthcare environment that could mean the difference between success and failure for these products.

Did you take your meds today? If so, you're ahead of a lot of people, because the problem of non-adherence - failure to take prescribed medications as directed - is killing 125,000 Americans annually[2], and costs the health care system nearly $300 billion a year in additional doctor visits, emergency department visits and hospitalizations[3]. Over 50% of patients just don't take their medications as prescribed – and that goes for everything from antidepressants to anti-seizure drugs. While this might be an economic issue for a lot of these patients, for many others it's a lot tougher to pin down a reason. Maybe the patient takes her antidepressants regularly for the first few weeks, then after a couple of months of feeling better, decides to drop them – which likely pitches her into a deeper depression. Maybe he doesn't use his inhaler properly, or forgets his meds for a couple of days then decides to double up to "make up" for it. Maybe she's not convinced of the medication's efficacy, or is worried about side effects she read about on the internet or is feeling, but doesn't want to discuss them with her provider. Whatever the reason, it's an issue we've failed to adequately address, so patients do not understand why it matters, and continue to put their health at risk. How do we get them to listen, and to appropriately take their medicine? How can we empower them to share their concerns about the medications they're prescribed with their healthcare providers? We've spent millions on these questions but if we can't come up with answers, at best, patients will not get the optimum benefit from their medicines, and at worst, many more lives could be lost unnecessarily.

A fascinating and potentially very serious problem is the notion of labeling disorders, syndromes or diseases without the appropriate analysis of how the label may affect individuals and our societies. Medicine has traditionally been siloed, as already mentioned. This has led to labels for diseases that may not be appropriate once the disease is better understood. Autism or Asperger's are examples in which the label is acquired early in a child's life, and sticks with them throughout their adulthood. Now that the idea of placing people on "the spectrum" for the disorder has been accepted as a way of categorizing these patients beyond what the official disease codes can offer. The potential for a disease's definition to become so broad as to be nearly all-inclusive is a significant challenge. Yet, there is no long-term view of how the original labels will affect those in the society with whom they interact or who care for them. This is especially troubling where there is no treatment for the syndrome, and society, for the most part, does not know how to integrate these children into the society as they grow up. There is a glaring need for Futuring here.

A related and rather large red herring that continues to create havoc in many communities was the vaccine autism scare, and the subsequent refusal of alarmed parents to have their children vaccinated. The release of a paper supposedly demonstrating the relationship of autism directly to childhood vaccines, along with celebrity endorsements of the theory, created a wave of distrust in childhood vaccines across many developed countries. As a result, thousands of children went without vaccines which is now resulting in the resurgence of several epidemic communicable diseases that have already included some deaths. At this writing, measles is making a comeback in communities scattered across the US, for instance. The data for the offending paper was eventually found to have been falsified, but by the time the publication was retracted, the damage was done. Red herrings can be powerful, and for some it can take a long time to undo the enthusiasm they can produce by seeming to answer a difficult question with a simple solution. For some parents, the red herring effect appears to have been irreversible.

Another good question for the future: What impact will climate change have on health, and how should we be preparing for it? Already we're seeing an uptick in mosquito-borne diseases in areas of the world where temperatures are rising. Global warming increases evaporation of surface water, which changes the balance in water distribution across the planet. As of this writing, changes in precipitation are creating extreme droughts in some areas and floods in others; the availability of drinking water is a problem for people in some areas, and rising waters and extreme weather events are displacing many others. Natural disasters driven by climate change – increasingly intense hurricanes, for instance – will create more health challenges in countries already struggling to establish basic sanitation systems.

Coastal flooding in sunny weather has become a new norm for Miami, and in November 2019, Venice, Italy experienced unprecedented floods. Coastlines worldwide are eroding, wildlife is changing, and diseases are evolving. According to a recent book by Bill McKibben, pollution kills more than 9 million people a year around the world, already more than malaria, TB and AIDS combined[4]. In Delhi, 4.4 million children were recently found to have irreversible lung damage from air pollution and by 2030 smog may claim more than 100 million lives. How can we act now, to mitigate not only climate change but to contain or soften its health impact going forward?

Want another ticking time bomb? According to information provided by the Alzheimer's Association, "As the size and proportion of the U.S. population age 65 and older continue to increase, the number of Americans with Alzheimer's or other dementias will grow. This number will escalate rapidly in coming years, as the population of Americans age 65 and older is projected to grow from 53 million in

2018 to 88 million by 2050. The baby boom generation has already begun to reach age 65 and beyond, the age range at greatest risk of Alzheimer's; in fact, the oldest members of the baby boom generation turned age 72 in 2018." Age-related dementia comes in many varieties in addition to Alzheimer's disease. Lewy Body dementia, most often found in those aged 50 or older, is the second most common type of dementia and includes features of Parkinson's disease and Alzheimer's. The disease is caused by multiple deposits of a protein called synuclein (the so-called Lewy bodies) in areas of the brain associated with sleep, movement, and decision-making. There is often overlap with Alzheimer's and Parkinson's disease pathology. However, the disease is distinct from Alzheimer's and brings its own challenges. Robin Williams, the beloved American actor and comedian, was diagnosed with Parkinson's disease before his suicide in 2014, but autopsy revealed he actually had Lewy Body dementia. His tragic loss may be related to the finding that one consequence of Lewy Body dementia is increased risk of suicide.

As life expectancy increases, many more people will be living with one type of dementia or another, and these people will need to be taken care of. With dementia at epidemic proportions, how will we house and treat those who have the disease? How can healthcare providers better use existing tools for early detection? There are genetic determinants of some forms of dementia, but until an effective treatment is available, what are the ethical challenges with advising individuals to be tested for these genes? A novel by Lisa Genova, adapted as a movie, *Still Alice*, addresses this ethical dilemma. Julianne Moore, in an award-winning turn as a linguistics professor and a mother with an inherited form of early onset Alzheimer's disease, knows she may have passed the gene to her children. Do they get tested or not? Two chose to know, the third opts not to. In one of her daughters, the gene test is positive; she will get the disease in her 50s or 60s. This particular gene is deterministic. How can we best support the families of those with the disease, and help them to cope with the stress of not only caring for a loved one with dementia, but also with the knowledge that they may also be at risk? Will assisted suicide or euthanasia become the accepted solutions for those at the end of what they consider their useful lives? Certainly, we're seeing some movement in that direction: In September of 2017, the Montreal Gazette reported,

"In the first study of its kind in Canada, an overwhelming majority of Quebec caregivers say they're in favour of extending medical assistance in dying to those afflicted with Alzheimer's disease or dementia.

The survey by Université de Sherbrooke epidemiologist Gina Bravo found that 91 percent of respondents support the idea of assisted dying for individuals suffering from dementia who are at the terminal state of their illness, showing signs of distress and who have an advance written directive. What's more, 72 percent said they were for assisted dying even for Alzheimer's patients who did not sign a written directive before their illness."

Futuring is needed on this topic to broaden thinking on how to deal with such a large percentage of the population being relatively robust, physically, but effectively crippled by cognitive deterioration. How might society need to change to accommodate these folks, and ensure a respectful, and comfortable existence as they live out their lives? Progressive thinking around care is happening: France, Denmark and the Netherlands have all been building Alzheimer's Villages that house patients and provide shops, entertainment, medical and social care, all on site. These are experimental but indicate a shift back towards institutional living, albeit of a very different kind, that the US moved away from during the 80s, when psychiatric patients were turned out of mental health facilities and into the street to "better integrate into the community" (and greatly increasing the homeless population in the process). In these new villages, those who are cognitively challenged are able to live in relative freedom, in a safe and reassuring environment. Communities like these are great experiments, and Futuring will help us imagine more options and keep the experiments coming.

End of life care is an issue that calls for Futuring; we're doing a fair to poor job now in terms of how we are failing to mitigate pain for those in the last stages of illness or to address the psychological challenges reported by people at the end of life, with depression, hopelessness, a painful sense of lost dignity and loneliness among them. Our healthcare workers are inadequately trained to deal with this population, and often undercompensated for the work they do. And while hospice is often the best solution at the very end, many who want to die at home can't get adequate support there to make that possible, and wind up dying in hospitals. The situation is only going to worsen as the aging population puts increasing stress on the imperfect systems we currently have in place. Part of the challenge is cultural; our medical system prizes length of life over quality of life, unlike, say, Japan, where the end is accepted as part of the inevitable cycle of life, and the focus is on the quality of one's remaining time rather than the quantity. Can Futuring help us to become both more humane and effectual in dealing with this issue? We believe it can, and must.

OTHER COMPLEX and interdisciplinary problems begging to be solved include:

- What impact will migration have on world health, as migrants flee wars, political upheaval or natural disasters? As climate change renders parts of the planet uninhabitable, who will accept the refugees, and how will it affect health patterns across the world?
- Given the ever-shrinking number of primary care physicians (PCPs), how will people in more remote locations be able to reliably access quality health care? According to a report published by the AAMC[5] (Association of American Medical Colleges) the United States will experience a shortfall of between 14,800 and

49,300 primary care physicians by 2030. One of us is directly experiencing the impact of this as of this writing: Sheryl lost her primary care physician when his practice became economically unviable and had to close down early this year. Finding a new PCP within a 20-mile radius of home who accepts new patients and who has appointments without a six-month wait has proved, so far, impossible.

- How will our health systems and society cope with the dearth of caretakers in a world where families no longer reliably live near each other? Increasingly we're seeing people in their middle years squeezed between the demands of work, children, and aging relatives – the "sandwich generation", as it's been dubbed. And those who are tasked with caring for relatives suffering from dementia are even more stressed; studies show[6] these overstressed adults suffer from depression, stress and anxiety.

- Experts warn that we're overdue for a massive flu pandemic, and that it's not so much as question of "if" as it is "when". The Spanish flu is estimated to have killed 50 million people in 1918. Flu killed and hospitalized more people in the United States during the 2017-2018 flu season than any seasonal influenza in decades, according to data released by the CDC, with a death toll of 80,000, according to an interview the director of the Centers for Disease Control and Prevention, Dr. Robert Redfield, gave to the Associated Press. How can we do better at predicting what strains of flu are the most likely to prevail in a given flu season – and how can we convince people to take the flu vaccine?

- How will the decisions being made by our governments now impact healthcare going forward? If ACA is repealed, how does this change the number of people in

the country who are insured and have access to care? What if ACA is reshaped and offers universal care? Does this impact the quality of care provided?
- What would happen if regulatory agencies decided to speed up approval of products? Would we see more benefit or risk? If they slow them down significantly, how many patients' lives would be lost? Does it become cost prohibitive to develop medicines due to the long time it takes for approval and the loss of patent length?
- How can we reverse current trends towards impersonal care due to overreliance on medication versus conversation, and further exacerbated by reliance on digital tools?
- We need more tangible advances in cancer diagnosis and treatment, because we've barely moved the needle in the last 30 years. Better treatments have extended patients' lives by just weeks in most cases. How can we do better for the millions of patients at risk, or diagnosed with cancer every day across the world?

These are all multifaceted problems – but if we work smarter at solving them, we believe that important progress can be made. That starts with putting our heads together: It will require input from leaders in multiple disciplines who are willing and able to put aside their own preconceptions and assumptions and work together to imagine multiple potential scenarios, what signposts might presage the advent of each of them, and how those changes might either support or hinder our efforts to move us in a better direction. Strategic planning can't accomplish this – but, done right, Futuring can.

IN ORDER TO FUTURE, you have to set today aside; to shift your mindset, to call upon an area of your brain to "imagine", because the imagined future is not connected to/dependent upon today. Futuring is not a sort of roleplaying science fiction; it isn't Star Trek or The Time Machine. But Futuring does allow us to move beyond our current assumptions to plausible stories and outcomes. Futuring helps us to anticipate the desired future and prepares us to address the challenges we're likely to face in that future, now, and to identify and to spot signposts that suggest we may be moving in a specific direction. Drivers and signposts are there, whether you see them or not. If you fail to recognize them, they won't trigger anything effective in terms of response. But if you do recognize them, you have an advantage, and can act to steer events (or your company's response) to survive the challenge. As former Shell Oil CEO Peter Voser put it, *"Scenarios provide the right framework for appreciating fundamental long-term choice, which is not the same as next year's annual plan."*

While the concept of Futuring may seem daunting, in fact it's a rewarding process, both for the company that spearheads it and for the participants. Futuring changes everything – including the thinking processes of the individuals who do it – for the better. It's ironic that how we think – that is, the way in which our brains are hard-wired to regard the future – is arguably the biggest reason most of us don't Future effectively - or at all.

Key points for Chapter Three

1. We need to make time to Future.
2. Futuring is a fundamental skill that resurrects the art of imagination, so easily accessed in childhood but often forsaken as we churn through the minutia of our adult lives.
3. The time is right for Futuring- and it is necessary for leaders at this time of great change and opportunity.
4. Silos are stifling. Futuring paves the way for competitive advantage by reaching across the divides and building

interdisciplinary contexts for solving our most challenging - and potentially rewarding - problems.
5. We are at a time of unprecedented potential. It would be a shame to waste it. Future Now!

---

1. Papanicolas I, Woskie LR, Jha AK. Health Care Spending in the United States and Other High Income Countries. JAMA.2018;319(10):1024–1039. doi:10.1001/jama.2018.1150
2. National Council on Patient Information and Education; Accelerating Progress in Prescription Medicine Adherence: The Adherence Action Agenda. A National-Action Plan to Address America's "Other Drug Problem." October 2013.
3. Iuga AO, McGuire MJ. Adherence and health care costs. Risk Management and Healthcare Policy. 2014;7:35-44. doi:10.2147/RMHP.S19801.
4. Bill McKibben; *Falter,* 2019. Pub Henry Holt and Company, New York NY
5. 2018 Update: The Complexities of Physician Supply and Demand: Projections from 2016 to 2030. The Association of American Medical Colleges: Dall, Tim Executive Director, West, Terry, Chakrabarti, Ritashree, Reynolds, Ryan, Iacobucci, Will
6. Solberg, L. M., Solberg, L. B., & Peterson, E. N. (2014). Measuring impact of stress in sandwich generation caring for demented parents. GeroPsych: The Journal of Gerontopsychology and Geriatric Psychiatry, 27(4), 171-179.

FOUR

HOW YOUR BRAIN RESISTS LOOKING AHEAD

"You are trying to manipulate people into being open-minded."
—Ted Newland, Shell manager of Long-Term Studies 1965–1971;
scenario team leader 1980–1981

In her best-selling book, *The Watchman's Rattle*, Rebecca A. Costa talks about how the growing list of complex and globally threatening challenges has expanded much more quickly than evolution has prepared our brain's ability to solve them, and posits a theory of how civilizations have fallen as a result. She draws a line from the collapse of the Mayan world to the threats currently faced by our own. The Mayans too struggled with climate change, and a crippling drought that overwhelmed their conservation efforts. Stymied in their efforts to engineer their way out of it, they retreated to their religious belief systems – beliefs that led to a years-long orgy of ritual human sacrifice. Within the span of a single generation, that centuries-old civilization simply disappeared:

"In the case of the Mayans, they became unable to "think" their way out of large, highly complex problems because they advanced to a point where traditional left- and right-brain problem-solving methods

– which the human organism developed over many millions of years – were no longer sufficient to address their most dangerous threats. Put another way, the intricacy and magnitude of the issues that the Mayans faced during their final hours – climate change, civil unrest food shortages, fast-spreading viruses, and a population explosion – exceeded their ability to obtain facts, analyze them, innovate, plan, and act to stop them. Their problems simply became too complex. The point at which a society can no longer "think" its way out of its problems is called the "cognitive threshold". And once a society reaches this cognitive threshold, it begins passing unresolved issues from one generation to the next until, finally, one or more of these problems push the civilization over the edge. This is the real reason for collapse... It seems irrational to assume that the left-and right-brain problem-solving methods we have evolved to this point have equipped us to address highly complex problems such as climate change, terrorism, pandemic viruses, and nuclear proliferation, especially since all of these problems share one obvious characteristic; they are multilayered, chaotic issues involving many, many variables acting in dynamic ways. In fact, our problems have become so large and so complex that experts rarely agree on what the problem is anymore..."

Costa's message is clear and unequivocal: Unless we're resigned to going the way of the Mayans, we have to do more to reach beyond our cognitive thresholds – to think bigger. Granted, we can't rush evolution, in the sense of rewiring our brains to work more effectively at problem solving (at least, not yet) – but we can expand our cognitive threshold by changing the framework in which we think – and Futuring provides us with the toolkit to do just that. That's the good news – and also the bad news. The mind shift required by Futuring is one of the reasons that it's so difficult for many people; we're literally not built to think that way.

RECENT RESEARCH[1] utilizing functional magnetic resonance imaging (fMRI) has shown that when we think about ourselves, a region of the brain called the medial prefrontal cortex (MPFC) fires up. When we think about other people, the region shuts down. When we think about ourselves in the future, the MPFC acts like we are thinking about someone else. In fact, the further out we imagine ourselves, the less our brain identifies that future person as us. It is as if a curtain gradually comes down on our view of ourselves now and ourselves in the future, the further out we go. The finding that we have trouble seeing ourselves in the future has implications for how we act in the present–if we don't identify with that future person who is us, then we aren't motivated to take actions now that might benefit our future selves. It offers an explanation for why we don't seem to care about climate change, or vaccination for diseases we can't envision contracting.

That cognitive disconnect is probably the simplest explanation for why most of us fail to save enough money to provide for our old age – it's so far away! – or to stick with a healthy diet or an exercise routine that would help us to enjoy a healthy old age. As the author Hal Hirshfield put it in his paper on the subject,

"Naturally, there will be less overlap between selves with a greater degree of temporal distance between them: with more time, psychological connectedness of oneself in the present with oneself in the future grows more tentative. People feel more connected to their potential self of five years than their potential self of forty years... What matters, for long-term planning, however, is that one person has but one identity, and it is with this link that the assets of the present and future selves are tied together. Individuals who feel as though the future self is a different person fail to acknowledge this connection, that is, fail to identify with themselves in the future."

A survey of 2,818 adults regarding how they viewed the future was done in 2017 by the Palo Alto-based Institute for the Future[2], and found:

"...more than a quarter of Americans rarely or never think about their lives five years from now; more than a third never think about something that could happen 10 years in the future; and more than

half of Americans rarely or never think about their lives 30 years out.

"We've got a 'future gap' in America," said Jane McGonigal, author of the survey and senior researcher at the Institute for the Future. "The majority of people aren't connecting with their future selves, which studies have shown leads to less self-control and less pro-social behavior. Thinking about the future in five, 10 and 30 years is essential to being an engaged citizen and creative problem solver. Curiosity about what might happen in the future, the ability to imagine how things could be different, and empathy for our future selves are all necessary if we want to create positive change in our own lives or the world around us."...Studies show the less people think about their future lives, the less self-control they exhibit and the less likely they are to make choices that benefit the world in the long run. People who don't think about the future vote less often, save less for retirement, make poor health decisions, procrastinate more, have a harder time resisting temptation, care less about long-term challenges like climate change, and are more likely to drop out of school or be arrested..."

Clearly, we need to be able to consider the future, at length and in depth, if we're going to be able to plan for it, influence it, and spot the indicators, or signposts, that suggest what's coming. As Jane McGonigal pointed out in an article for Slate, "No one can predict the future, but plenty of people are out there talking about what the future could be—with new technologies, new policies, new culture. And when you can imagine concrete details of a possible future, it's easier to close the future gap and put yourself into that future. Future you becomes less of a stranger—and someone you can actively conspire on behalf of to create a better world and a better life."

Again, this holds true in no area more greatly than it does in healthcare, where our success or failure not only as creators and providers of therapies and medications hinges on connecting with and foreseeing the needs of "future you", and influencing behaviors.

> *"This research is supportive of the modern-day dilemma we are in; where we are creating our "now" in the form of the "on demand" economy that keeps our neurologic pathways lit up with the jolts of endorphins and dopamine we get from all that available gratification." - Kelly*

ANOTHER STUDY from researchers in the UK and New Zealand[3] showed that the ability to imagine the future is associated with cognitive flexibility as well as functional semantic memory (the ability to remember facts and figures irrespective of personal experience). It's curious that we need the past to envision the future. In fact, cognition and semantic memory provide the neural framework to allow humans to Future.

The Institute for the Future say it is not difficult to get into the habit of Futuring and teaches its student to do just that by asking them to think of their favorite things and then Google the future of those things. In their view, this gives people a concrete picture of a possible future and makes it easier to close that gap between themselves in the present and themselves in the future.

For us, Futuring requires thought, intention, effort, skill and eventually action to produce the desired behavioral shift towards the future thinking habit. Ideally, all pieces need to be in place if the Futuring habit is to be sustainable.

The Tale of the Immunologist's Wife

You might imagine that those who are presented with evidence from trusted sources about how critical it is to be prepared for the future would be good at making smart decisions about it, but in at least one case we know of, that wasn't true.

Dr. X is a well-known immunologist, highly respected in his field, and obviously well aware of the benefits of immunization. So, when the shingles vaccine first became available, he told his wife that she needed to be vaccinated. She was over fifty years old, and had had chicken pox as a child. Shingles is an extremely painful condition that results from a reactivation of the chickenpox virus and that can lead to all kinds of awful complications, like vision loss and neurological impairment. According to the Centers for Disease Control, about one in three adults will have shingles at some time in their lives, and until it happens, most have no idea about the seriousness of the disease. The doctor wanted his wife to take what were in his view appropriate precautions.

But his wife had no interest in getting the vaccine; to her, the notion of getting shingles seemed to be a distant, barely meaningful threat. Wasn't that something that only happened to old people? She had no personal experience with the condition; nobody she knew had ever had shingles, and so she believed the chances of her developing it were slim. Still, because he loved her – and because he believed in the effectiveness of vaccines - her husband continued to bring it up on a regular basis, and just as reliably, she continued to ignore him – right up to the day that one of the women in her walking group came down with a hideous, agonizing case of shingles.

Suddenly she and the rest of her group were lining up to get the vaccine. Why? The reality of shingles and the suffering she could see it inflicting on her friend became part of her reality, so her thinking about it, and her belief system, shifted accordingly. Facts didn't matter. Experience did.

Do we, as healthcare innovators, want to be like the immunologist's wife, yoked to a belief system that limits our worldview to just that which we ourselves have seen or experienced? More to the point, can we afford to be? We think not. But all of us are in thrall to our beliefs, to a greater or lesser extent, and so thoroughly do they color and shape our world view that we're largely unconscious of them as being "beliefs" at all, in the sense of potentially artificial constructs influenced by our experience or what we've been taught. Rather, we see them as inarguable fact. This friction between belief and, say, scientific truth, is all around us, though – and it's not limited to people whose world views are parochial or narrow-minded. We all live, work, and make judgments and decisions from inside our individual cages of belief; it's just that it's easier to see the bars on the other guy's, because we're peering out from between the bars on our own.

Another story about vaccination – and the fears that have grown up around it, particularly in the last ten or so years – illustrates that tension very clearly. Science writer Erik Vance[4] blogged about the power of fear and how easily it trumps rational thought – even for someone whose whole career has been built on understanding and explaining science. Everything he knew about vaccines – that they're safe, effective, and necessary – went out the window when it was time for his 18-month-old-son to get his vaccinations against diphtheria, meningitis, whooping cough and tetanus. Suddenly, all the pseudo-scientific alarmism he'd shrugged off in the past came rushing at him, and he nearly faltered when it came time to hold his son still for his shots. In the piece, Vance describes himself as a man of science – or at least, as someone who's more knowledgeable about and invested in science than most people, then says,

"Which is why it was weird when I took my infant son in for his first vaccines and started peppering his pediatrician with questions. I inspected the boxes, telling myself that I was concerned about a recent bad batch of vaccines in Chiapas, Mexico, that made a bunch of kids sick. But really, I was looking for a label that read "not the autism kind of vaccine."

"I felt really uncomfortable and started to sweat. I looked at the clear liquid in the vials and wondered, will I regret this for the rest of my life? I started to think about maybe delaying the injections until it was safer or maybe stretching them out over a longer period of time. I mean, it just can't be safe giving all these vaccines at once.

Seriously? I've spent years following the vaccine safety debate, reading the stories and writing a few stories about how safe and effective vaccines are. And yet here I am putting my entire profession to

disgrace, just as scared and confused as anyone else. In that moment, I wanted to slap my brain upside the temporal lobe. The sight of one little needle was turning me into a raging anti-vaxxer."

He was able to go through with the vaccinations, despite his moment of panic and guilt, but asks,

"If fear is more powerful than hope and this could happen to a fundamentally rational person like me, then what hope does science really have? What chance does "This is a well-studied, safe intervention" have against "Holy s***, I might be ruining my child!"?

Now go beyond that to other issues where fears and tribal loyalties conflict with reason, like GMOs, climate change or evolution. How can rationality win when irrationality is so much more attractive? I sat in the doctor's office staring into space, now terrified of something totally different."

Beliefs exist to protect us from what we fear; that loss of control that challenges our egos and fills us with a primordial terror that must be very like what our early ancestors experienced when something large and hungry roared from beyond the comforting spill of the firelight. We weave webs of beliefs to sustain us in the face of existential dread, to armor us against a hostile and still in many ways, unknowable universe. Beliefs put control – or the illusion of it – back into our hands, and give us back the agency that chaos has stolen.

Does the evidence of man-made climate change frighten us? We come up with alternative "science" to explain it away. Does a grim diagnosis strip us of reasonable hope? We put ourselves in the hands of alternative practitioners, subjecting ourselves to "cures" with no track records for success, rather than accepting the inevitable – yes, even if we're as brilliant and forward-thinking as Steve Jobs, because death is the great leveler, and the echo of its pitiless roar roiling out from the darkness reduces us all to naked, shivering cave dwellers.

Mankind has spent most of its existence going to war - or to press - over closely held, conflicting beliefs. Take religious faith versus atheism, for instance. Coming down on one side or another is certainly beyond the purview of this book, but in his book, *What If We're*

Wrong?[5], author Chuck Klosterman makes a good case for not taking a side in what has surely been humanity's most contentious and long-standing argument: whether or not there's any sort of life after death. As he points out in his thought-provoking (and for some readers, just plain provoking) book,

"*When considered rationally, there is no justification for believing that anything happens to anyone upon the moment of his or her death. There is no reasonable counter to the prospect of nothingness. Any anecdotal story about "floating toward a white light" or Shirley MacLaine's past life on Atlantis or the details in <u>Heaven Is for Real</u> are automatically (and justifiably) dismissed by any secular intellectual. Yet this wholly logical position discounts the overwhelming likelihood that we currently don't know something critical about the experience of life, much less the ultimate conclusion to the experience.*

There are so many things we don't know about energy, or the way energy is transferred, or why energy (which can't be created or destroyed) exists at all. We can't truly conceive the conditions of a multidimensional reality, even though we're (probably) already living inside one. We have a limited understanding of consciousness. We have a limited understanding of time, and of the perception of time, and of the possibility that all time is happening at once. So, while it seems unrealistic to seriously consider the prospect of life after death, it seems equally naïve to assume that our contemporary understanding of this phenomenon is remotely complete. We have no idea what we don't know, or what we'll eventually learn, or what might be true despite our perpetual inability to comprehend what that truth is.

It's impossible to understand the world of today until today has become tomorrow."

In examining the public's denial of scientific knowledge – whether that's around the purported "dangers" of vaccines versus their life-saving capabilities, or the threat of climate change, authors[6] Sara E. Gorman, PhD, MPH and Jack M. Gorman, MD identify six important, arguably inborn, tendencies that make it more challenging to separate facts from beliefs.

1. *Conspiracy*: We tend to buy into conspiracy theories, at least in part because occasionally they're true. On other occasions, however, they're not, as in the broadly popular idea that vaccines are an elaborate con job in which Big Pharma, Big Medicine, etc., have "financed a cadre of scientists with impressive credentials to promote false and misleading science..." in order to reap obscene profits.
2. *Charismatic Leaders* are those whose stated mission is to expose these conspiracies - and whose powerful personalities and "expertise" work together to convince the unwary that they're telling the truth.
3. *Confirmation Bias:* We're inclined to accept new information only when it conforms to what we already believe to be true, and to ignore or discredit whatever conflicts with what we "know". We actively choose not to pay attention to this conflicting information. The authors point out that this is "strongly rooted in primitive needs and emotion" – the need for a sense of control in a reckless and dangerous world – and not amenable to correction merely by reciting facts.
4. *Causality and Filling the Ignorance Gap*: People are inclined to attribute causality where it doesn't exist, because they're uncomfortable with not knowing the reason for a thing, and are unable to deal with that uncertainty. While making causal inference, leaping to conclusions is how we protect ourselves from that uncertainty. This, they suggest, is the reason why the layperson will demand antibiotics for a cold, even when they're told it won't help and in fact might do damage.
5. *Avoidance of Complexity*: Modern science is complex, its language full of jargon and knotty concepts that make it impenetrable to laypeople. It's easy to tune it out, because

it's so hard to wade through the weeds of the scientific method.
6. *Risk Perception and Probability:* Like the immunologist's wife, we generally hold an overly-optimistic view of our own level of risk, often based on a defective understanding of probability - and that's further complicated by the underlying beliefs (true or not) that dictate our perception of our risk, which is often far different than the actual, measurable risk involved.

CLEARLY, changing our beliefs is heavy lifting; they come fully charged with emotion, and challenging them can be seen as a challenge to the person, rather than the idea, so there's built-in resistance. Yet for all the comfort their assurances offer in an uncertain world, they do limit us – and if we're to move forward, we've got to be able to take them apart, examine their component parts and shed those that no longer seem tenable once they've been viewed in bright daylight.

And it can be done. Within our lifetimes we've seen many beliefs that held us captive to a less inclusive model of society, for instance, have been changed within individuals when they were exposed to new experiences that conflicted with what they'd been taught. What keeps us from thinking in a more disruptive, creative way generally?

One explanation is that we are all repositories of old assumptions, and we carry them around with us. In order to think disruptively, we need to shift the assumptions which means we have to shift our beliefs – and that's tough. We've seen again and again in healthcare that simply making a reasoned medical argument for something isn't enough to do it. As we've said, simply telling someone that they need to take their medication as prescribed isn't enough to ensure their adherence. To create a real shift, something has to challenge the beliefs patients already hold.

Another piece is that we're often engaged in solving the wrong problem, or going at the right problem from the wrong direction. That's usually due to our faulty assumptions; we're trying to solve for something that's not necessarily solvable. But people who are really good at disruption – at innovation – see a different problem, or see it differently.

Why, for instance, do we underutilize vaccines but overuse antibiotics? How can we help people to properly understand the dangers of antibiotic resistance? We were in a discussion recently with a woman whose task it is to try and solve this problem, and she explained the challenge as she sees it: People believe they know their own body better than their doctor does, and will go into the doctor's office and demand an antibiotic. Even if the doctor tells the patient that what he has is a viral infection, not a bacterial one, and antibiotics won't help, what the patient knows is that when he's been sick in the past with something that felt like what he's feeling now, an antibiotic worked – and he wants one.

What's frustrating for people trying to educate the public about this is that even though people are very willing intellectually to entertain the facts around the dangers of antibiotic abuse, and willing to hear about and discuss it rationally, when push comes to shove and they're in the doctor's office, they will override the doctor's advice and demand antibiotics. Her conclusion was that unless you do something substantive to change their beliefs/assumptions, it doesn't matter how many factsheets or commercials or magazine articles you put in front of them, or how well received they are, the change in behavior just doesn't happen.

One tool that's recently come back into fashion for better understanding and affecting these kinds of behaviors is ethnographic research. Rather than just asking a patient questions or offering them information, ethnographic researchers attempt to understand people and how they live. If you are researching adherence, for instance, you would probably want to know where in their homes people store their medications. Are they in the back of the medicine cabinet? On their bedside table? Or are they mixed in with the bottles of supplements on the kitchen counter?

If you're doing research (as one of us, was some years back) on how to help people at risk for macular degeneration to remember to regularly test their eyesight, you have to make sure the test is something they'll actually look at. Doctors give people at risk – typically the elderly -a sheet of paper on which what's called the Amsler Grid is printed; used regularly, it can help patients do their own early diagnosis of changes in their vision. It's a great tool when you use it – but the problem was that people were sticking it up on the fridge so it was becoming part of the furniture, in the sense that they just stopped noticing it was there – and stopped checking their vision.

An alternative idea was proposed when, during the course of research, it was observed that older people are often enthusiastic consumers of puzzle books for entertainment and for mental exercise. The solution was to give the elderly person a book of word or math puzzles – a book that that they'll reliably pick up every day – with an Amsler Grid printed on the last page, and put a reminder at the bottom of each page to go to the back of the book and test their eyes. This actually improved compliance markedly. The point is, understanding how people actually live, and what they do in their day to day lives, helps us understand ways in which we can change their behavior that are much more effective.

"Thinking disruptively – examining a question from a very different angle – is a skill we believe can be developed." - Kelly

---

THINKING DISRUPTIVELY IS an essential skill for solving the

otherwise insoluble problems we wrestle with in healthcare. But it takes a fresh perspective – and that's a hard thing to come by in our day-to-day lives, especially since so much about the modern world works against it.

Be honest: How much energy do you put into challenging your beliefs, whether that's by reading a book written by someone whose views are opposite to yours, or even by maintaining relationships in which the other person's ideas are in conflict with yours? It's tempting to slip into the comfortable habit of seeking out confirmation bias rather than looking for challenges, especially since social media makes it so easy to simply mute anything we find offensive or beyond the perimeters we've set for what we accept as true. We talk to like-minded people, we read like-minded authors, we watch like-minded entertainment, and we begin to imagine that our perspective is the only one worth holding. We call this the bubble – but really, it's the cage.

Futuring gives us the chance to swing open the cage door, letting us view our existing beliefs from a fresh perspective. That puts us back in the driver's seat to decide whether those beliefs are relevant and true, or need to be reassessed.

Futuring lets you pause in a world that can't stop moving

How often during the day do you check your phone, your emails, Twitter, Instagram or your Facebook page? These are all good and useful activities in their way, but the rush of right-now gratification and comfort they give us gets in the way of the open-ended imaginative thinking we need to make time to do. That's because for most of us, the skills needed to future are often lost to adulthood. Children are fearless and innocent because they lack developed beliefs in many areas. They have little working knowledge, so beliefs aren't ingrained because experiences haven't happened yet. The tendency to imagine is strong and essential to navigating a world that is unfolding before them. Even though we often lose the skill, we've seen that it can be re-learned. If a purposeful pause is created to make the space to think about a challenging problem, even people who are less in touch with that set of creative functions can find themselves thinking differently as the process unfolds. Giving our colleagues and ourselves permission to simply put the world we live in on "pause" over the course of a few hours or days creates room for visionary thought, inspiration and new ways to look at the world.

If your initial reaction to the idea of Futuring is somewhere between a shoulder shrug - "Why should I?" - and an eye roll - "Why would I?" - you're not alone. In fact, some iteration of those responses is what we typically see when Futuring is proposed to those who have not engaged in Futuring before. But, apart from the most obdurate "now-ists" who simply refuse to make room in their heads for anything not immediately concrete and provable, and who see the exercise of imagination as a waste of time, everyone we've Futured with has come out of it excited by the possibilities it raises, and galvanized by the recognition of their own newfound abilities.

Greater clarity about their organization's potential role in the future emerges, as do practical strategies for improved influence and viability in the marketplace. And beyond those immediate benefits, new professional alliances are created across multiple disciplines as people interact in this special setting, alliances that have led to fruitful collaborations and partnerships apart from the Futuring itself. Futuring expands not only your view of the world as it might be, but as it is – and the larger potentials that may exist in it for your enterprise.

And if you're still skeptical, consider that when the idea of mindfulness was first introduced to the west by Dr. Jon Kabat-Zinn in 1979, his Mindfulness-Based Stress Reduction (MBSR) Program at the University of Massachusetts Medical School was treated as a pop-psych, quick-fix, touchy-feely Buddhism Lite, not as a serious therapeutic tool. Time has proved him right, and his skeptics wrong, and mindfulness has become mainstream with multiple studies showing it measurably relieves stress and reduces depression.

Like mindfulness, Futuring is tough to describe or to practice if you haven't done it before, but brings multiple benefits to those willing to try it.

Like mindfulness, Futuring frees you to pause, think, and imagine. If you think you're already using your full cognitive capacity, it helps you to push past those limits and discover more. Those who don't Future are stuck approaching it from one direction – the now – and reacting to it, rather than acting upon it.

Futuring doesn't require you to set aside your beliefs before jumping in. You bring them with you into the room, and into a group setting; all that's really required is that you be open to the possibility of having those beliefs altered, shifted, emphasized or rejected. It's a transformative experience, and because it's shared in a social way with your colleagues, it connects you to a bigger, more powerful experience. The strength of the group transformation, in which you share interest with a group of varied stakeholders, is what creates the powerful community of cause. And that community can take your efforts beyond the confines of the Futuring, inspiring activism and collectivism around that shared goal.

"What we've found at every single one of these Futuring experiences is that, halfway through the day, there are already people talking about how they can get together to move forward with the big ideas they've come up with. There's an excitement around it, and a drive to commit to future collaboration as the people get into that Futuring mindset." - Erin

---

It's transformative. It's fun. *And it works.*

Key points for Chapter Four:

1. While the scope of the challenges we face today demands

that we learn to think differently, we're hard-wired to resist doing so.
2. Our belief systems can cause us to reject facts over feelings.
3. The silos in which we work prevent us from getting a clear view of the true scope and size of a problem.
4. Futuring creates an opportunity to push past our usual way of seeing and thinking, and to expand our cognitive thresholds.

---

1. Hershfield, Hal. (2011). Future self-continuity: How conceptions of the future selftransform intertemporal choice. Annals of the New York Academy of Sciences. 1235. 30-43. 10.1111/j.1749-6632.2011.06201.x.
2. McGonigal, Jane: "The American Future Gap", IFTF.com http://www.iftf.org/fileadmin/user_upload/downloads/IFTF_TheAmericanFutureGap_Survey_SR-1948.pdf (Accessed August 6, 2018)
3. Neuropsychologia. 2017 Jan 27;95:156-172. doi: 10.1016/j.neuropsychologia.2016.11.019. Epub 2016 Nov 28.: An fMRI investigation of the relationship between future imagination and cognitive flexibility. Roberts RP, Wiebels K, Sumner RL, van Mulukom V, Grady CL, Schacter DL, Addis DR
4. https://www.npr.org/sections/health-shots/2017/06/10/532110787/a-dad-takes-his-son-to-the-doctor-and-discovers-fear-of-vaccines
5. Chuck Klosterman, *But What If We're Wrong?* 2016, Blue Rider Press
6. Sara E Gorman, PhD, MPH and Jack M. Gorman, MD.: Denying to the Grave: Why We Ignore the Facts that Will Save Us: Oxford University Press, 2016, MD Oxford University Press, 2016

SECTION TWO: HOW TO FUTURE

FIVE
LAY THE GROUNDWORK
DARE TO DISRUPT

Thorough preparation is arguably the most critical aspect of productive Futuring – and the point at which many people that try to Future will fail.

Some of the questions you need to weigh as you consider and begin to prepare for Futuring are:

- Do you have a goal that might be accomplished or a problem that could be solved by Futuring? Solving a product manufacturing challenge may not be, for instance – but shaping a new market for that product in the future certainly is. It will be essential to understand the market into which you will launch your product, even if it is a decade or more away.
- Do you have buy-in from the right people internally to be sure you can secure the budget and have a receptive audience for the outcome?
- Do others in your organization share your interest in reaching that goal or solving that problem? Or are their

views of what the issue is very different than yours, because of where they sit in the organization?
- What's the level of tolerance for disruption for you, and the leadership within your organization? An honest assessment of this has to be infused into your planning before you move forward. If there is a vision of disruption and an appetite for innovation and transformation, then Futuring may be the catalyst to begin in all three areas.
- Do you have the fortitude and vision to be a leader in the marketplace - to make change, versus just selling your product? Can you make the commitment to disrupt, and to what degree?
- Are you brave enough to do this? This is important because to get this off the ground, you're going to have to argue for its value up and down the chain in your organization, since Futuring is different from the way in which most organizations function. It's likely to be a hard sell, because the notion of Futuring won't light anyone's neurons up. They're focused on more immediate stuff.
- Lastly, do you have a story? We strongly encourage those involved in preparing at this point to think through their story – what they'll tell their colleagues and their superiors about what they hope to accomplish and how. An elevator version is the real test. If you find you can't come up with a coherent story, you're probably not sufficiently prepared for Futuring.

Define your issue

The first piece of actual preparation for your Futuring is defining your issue – and that's an easy place to go off the rails, because the temptations are either to make the central question too broad in its scope, or too narrow. You need to get clarity about what you want to accomplish, what you can accomplish, and to decide how broad you want to be. Is your goal to solve global challenges in the world of healthcare, or do you just want to crack one little piece of it? Do you want to lead the field, or be the best at what you do? When we start exploring this territory with our pharma clients, we typically hear responses like, "We need to get better uptake on vaccines" or "I want to get more people to use this drug". It is rare that we hear, right off the bat, "I want to change the way we think about managing this disease".

In one sense, the optimal place to begin is to consider the current environment, and what you need to achieve. What's your identity now, versus what you want it to be in the future? What are your goals, and the associated unknowns? What are the factors that could stop you from accomplishing that goal? What could conceivably help you? That's where we begin to get a real sense of the breadth of the problem we're looking to solve. You can often end up redefining your goals too as you go through that process. Thinking in this way, starting from the present and projecting forward, means you carry all your current assumptions into your future. However, if you can start with the end in mind, then work back toward the current landscape, you have the opportunity to challenge your current assumptions and come up with a more disruptive role for you, your company, or your product in the future.

Without making value judgments, you need to be able to honestly define how big you want to go. For instance, if you're a major oil company, do you simply want to sell more oil than your competitors - or do you want to become the leader in alternative energy sources?

Leadership means different things in different contexts, and defining it clearly helps you to determine the boundaries of your scenarios. How much influence do you want to wield beyond your own company or industry? Do you want to take actions that will benefit the larger world – or do you want to benefit your own organization only?

> *"This is the kind of conversation you have to have upfront as you define your questions. If your goal is to just sell more oil or more medicines, you are not going to be disruptive. If you want to be a leader in alternative energy, or in new ways of treating cancer, then you are going to have be disruptive and you need to be prepared to take that on."* - Erin

TO FORMULATE a question that hits the "just right" sweet spot of scope, you're going to need input from those within your organization; a small internal group built around what we call the "problem owners". Begin by getting input from these internal stakeholders; what do they and you see as the burning questions or issues that you need to address on the horizon? Let's say you've got a new slate of medications that are planned for launch in 2030 or later: The question might be, "What can we do to insure that, when they do come out, people will take them?" Note that this question includes related questions such as "Will physicians prescribe the drug?", but doesn't address (nor is it meant to) ancillary questions that concern aspects over which you have no control, like, "What if the medications fail clinical trials?" because that's not solvable in this context.

What do you need to know about the environment surrounding your question or issue that might impact your ability to accomplish your aim – for instance, getting more doctors to prescribe your drug? Answers we often hear to this question are:

- "We need to know what the healthcare system will look like in ten years, because if people can't get or afford our drug, they can't take it."
- "Will we be able to get buy-in from doctors? If they don't believe it works, they're not going to prescribe it."
- "If patients don't want it, they won't take it."

- "If the science isn't there to support it, we might not be able to do the studies we want to do."

What impacts the world of healthcare, and where your company fits into it? What might contribute to your company's ability to impact those things, or to act to keep you from changing them? Those factors might include politics, the economics of healthcare, and natural or man-made disasters. This is where you start to consider the breadth of the problem you want to solve.

Whether it's a vaccine, a procedure or a new therapy, it's a missed opportunity and a poor use of resources for your company to come up with a great product and put it on the market in an environment in which consumers don't believe that what you're treating or preventing is a real disease or threat.

What is your organization's tolerance for disruption?

We've talked about the organization's tolerance for or appetite for disruption, but how can you optimize the chances that the organization will agree with your desire for disruption?

In formulating your questions, you have to honestly assess the culture of your company, and its openness to taking on disruptive, innovative multi-year initiatives. You know your colleagues: Will your corporate culture support bigger, more challenging thinking? If it will not, then the scope of your question has to be narrowed and focused, and the problem you're going to solve has to be tied more specifically to your product. This is where having a compelling and well-crafted narrative is crucial to getting buy-in. Is there a willingness to shake off conventional assumptions, and to lead the field?

If the answer is yes – do you want to take actions that just benefit your company, or do you want to raise all ships? Being a leader requires courage, and the willingness to go there changes how you approach the Futuring. As Futurists, we see people tend to narrow-focus too much, spending excessive bandwidth on the short term, and holding onto short-term objectives. We also see difficulty with imaging a future scope that is potentially much broader than that in which the field operates today. In the future, there will certainly be different players in your space and those possibilities will not be captured if the thinking is too narrow and bounded by our stakeholders today. We'll talk more about that when we discuss who you'll want to invite to Future with you.

While there are no "right" answers, and you're certainly not required to put either yourself or your organization out on a ledge, this is the value in Futuring. There's no safer place to explore the possibilities, and in our experience the organizations who get the most out of this are those who are bold enough to push the limits, and think bigger. More often than not, and maybe more importantly, it's also true that whatever your personal or corporate tolerance for disruption may be before you Future, our experience is that it's very likely to be expanded by Futuring.

Pharma Alpha, who you remember was a large company with a deep desire to disrupt the diabetes space, had two very dynamic and forward-thinking people leading the charge for the Futuring project: Their "go for it" attitude informed not just the scope of the Futuring, which took place over several days on a couple of continents, but their commitment to following up on what they'd gleaned over the long term, and cultivating productive cross-silo and interdisciplinary partnerships to consider the impacts to their business today.

Where does my goal live?

Once you've defined what it is you want to explore, you have to do a deep dive into the environment within which the problem exists. This requires creating the environmental landscape – what we call the landscape assessment. This is a research project that will necessarily take you out of the silo you're in, and have you peeking down into other, unfamiliar silos – other disciplines, specialties, businesses, academic settings, research results, organizations, urban planners etc.

– for insights and data that let you draw the big-picture, 360-degree view for your Futuring stakeholders.

That begins with where you are right now. Whatever it is your company does, and whatever industry you're in, in creating a landscape we start with a broad assessment of where it is in the present, whether that's countrywide or worldwide. What is the state of your industrial environment as it stands today?

If we're talking about healthcare in the United States, for instance, you'd have to say that the infrastructure of the system within which it's provided is currently unstable and in a state of flux. You'd look at the ACA as it stands; how it's being discussed, amended, or potentially abolished, and how effective it is in its current form. Who would be affected if it went away and what is being discussed to replace it? You would include some research on digital health; how is it being deployed now, what is it capable of, and how widely is it being used? You would likely include perceptions of the utility of digital health from the perspective of various stakeholders; whether it is their view that it is delivering on the promise, or that it's falling short, and why they see it that way. If you're looking at the market for a medicine you're developing, what are the attitudes of physicians currently toward the disease or condition your medication is intended to treat? The landscape view should include observations regarding factual information, as well as perceptions from across the field. Perceptions can make or break a product launch, just as easily as they can break or mend a relationship. It's important to know where everything stands in the "now".

How does this look in action? In the case of Pharma Alpha who was investigating market readiness for their new diabetes drug, we reviewed the broad landscape regarding healthcare and endocrine disease. Our landscape was broad because diabetes is often part of a complex spectrum of disease call metabolic syndrome, a condition that touches virtually every bodily system.

Diabetes research is very active, and researchers are gleaning significant learning from successful new target mechanisms for treatment. The understanding of the disease is deepening and broadening, so the market for products with which to treat it is likely to be very different in ten years. While this an exciting and dynamic clinical area, on the consumer side, pharma struggles to achieve treatment goals in this population, and there are many possible reasons why.

Some of the challenges we found were:

- Diagnosis is often delayed.
- Delivery of treatments is inconsistent.
- Access to some treatments is unreliable.
- Public ignorance of the risks, coupled with lifestyle challenges sets back progress for the diagnosis and treatment of some aspects of the disease. Take heart attacks, for instance, the risk for which is elevated in patients with diabetes. In recent years, heart disease has been on the decline thanks to years of public health efforts and widespread education campaigns. However, heart disease is making a comeback because we have become somewhat complacent, not to mention more sedentary as we sit glued to our screens more and more each day.
- Indifference to diabetes from the treating community; the triggers to treat are often nebulous.
- Patients often fail to see themselves as being at risk (like the immunologist's wife).
- Affordability is a barrier across the globe.
- Implementation is hampered by ineffective partnerships across sectors.

For Pharma Alpha's landscape assessment, we covered the rate of diabetes in the United States and Europe, and explored some of the social forces impacting those numbers: What currently prevents those who have the disease from getting diagnosed? What does research tell us can influence the thinking of those who do not take their blood sugar seriously? What are the challenges the marketplace presents, in terms of costs of treatment and who will cover them? How is diabetes currently treated and by whom? The treatment landscape is changing as more doctors delegate to nursing professionals, and the primary care physician finds himself with less time to spend with the patient and more with the electronic health record. Add a pressure to perform interventions that bring in more money, versus just prescribing a pill, and we see a shifting landscape full of hurdles for the doctor/patient relationship.

We looked at the specific disease's status; who is treating it and how, and how those therapies are performing. How is elderly health in general developing, given that type 2 diabetes is often a disease of middle and old age? What's happening on the tech side? What's going on in digital health?

The point of this wide-angle landscape assessment is that it helps us to better understand what challenges we're facing in the now, and thus what we're going to want to address in our Futuring. For it to be fruitful, we have to bring that thinking back to today and the environment that we've described. That shared view of where we are today is how we decide how we want to use the information and the thinking that we've derived from Futuring.

Let's use digital health as an example, because while it's creating a lot of buzz, there's some resistance to it from physicians, who don't generally take the patient-derived data all that seriously. Why? The advent of computer data collection means that doctors must spend more and more time looking at their screens, rather than at their patients, and using their valuable and limited time learning how to wrangle complex and ever-changing software, when they want to be seeing patients. As Dr. Atul Gawande said in the *New Yorker*,[1]

"I've come to feel that a system that promised to increase my mastery over my work has, instead, increased my work's mastery over me. I'm not the only one. A 2016 study found that physicians spent about two hours doing computer work for every hour spent face to face

with a patient—whatever the brand of medical software. In the examination room, physicians devoted half of their patient time facing the screen to do electronic tasks. And these tasks were spilling over after hours. The University of Wisconsin found that the average workday for its family physicians had grown to eleven and a half hours. The result has been epidemic levels of burnout among clinicians. Forty percent screen positive for depression, and seven percent report suicidal thinking—almost double the rate of the general working population.

Something's gone terribly wrong. Some doctors are among the most technology-avid people in society; computerization has simplified tasks in many industries. Yet, somehow, we've reached a point where people in the medical profession actively, viscerally, volubly hate their computers."

If a critical piece of the future you want is that health care is going to depend on real-time collection of data by doctors so that they can see on a day-to-day basis how a patient's health is faring, when within that environment today physicians are increasingly resistant to being tied to their laptops, you know you have work to do, today, to make that viable in the future. Thus, one of the strategic pillars you identify through Futuring could be creating a more simplified and manageable approach for physicians to access and use their patient's data.

THIS LANDSCAPE ASSESSMENT provides you with your starting point; it helps you to figure out what you could do to take that starting point and evolve it to shape the future that you want, so its breadth and accuracy are critical to its value. Don't skimp on this research, because it underpins everything that follows.

This research also lays the foundation for determining the stakeholders, and who you'll ultimately choose as participants for your Futuring.

Key points for Chapter 5

1. Define the issue your Futuring is going to address.
2. Decide to disrupt (You need to be proactive; take a stand!).
3. Create a view of the "now" that you feel comfortable sharing.
4. Establish the time and place for Futuring.

---

1. Gawande, Atul: Why Doctors Hate Their Computers, The New Yorker, Nov. 12, 2018

SIX
CHOOSING YOUR FUTURISTS

How many people will you Future with – and who will they be? Determining the number of people in the room is critical to successful Futuring, as is putting together the best available group of experts whose special knowledge speaks to a component of your problem.

Our experience suggests that the key to populating your group is to stick with numbers that encourage, rather than inhibit, participation by the individual, while at the same time having enough participants to have full representation of your key topic areas with each of your breakout groups. We've experimented with different sized groups, and have found that the optimal size is no fewer than eight and no more than fifteen in each breakout – and the sweet spot for us is the dirty dozen.

Why? It's a partly question of group dynamics and partly a question of how comfortable your Futurists will be with diverse topics and multiple voices in a short space of time. Selection of individuals who will be happy holding several contradictory and possibly competing thoughts in their minds at one time will be essential to success of the conversation. If you have just five people in the room, a leader will almost certainly emerge and take control of the conversation, or at least try to sway the group's thinking. If this leader has trouble with contradictory concepts (for example, "universal healthcare is essential for future health" versus "universal healthcare will never be possible because we are culturally and economically opposed"), they will become trapped into dogmatic lines of discussion pretty quickly, and will drag everyone along with them. This could limit the breadth of discussion you have if you only have five people in the group.

> *"You can Future with bigger groups, as long as you break them down into smaller groups to go through exercises. If a client wanted to include sixty people, for instance, we'd set up a construct of breaking the large group up into four groups of fifteen each, then leading those smaller groups through the Futuring scenarios."* - Kelly

Considering that the future you imagine should be broad enough to account for disruption at the edges of your space, you need to be sure you have enough of your key disciplines in the room and the right personalities to allow the possibilities to emerge. More voices are therefore ideal. If you have fifteen people in the group, multiple leaders are likely to emerge – and they're less likely to be able to stifle contrarian opinions. The problem we've found with having more than fifteen in a group is that certain kinds of personalities just shut down and don't participate when the group gets that big; typically, introverts will retreat into silence, and you'll lose their contributions.

> *"It's been interesting to see that when we take two groups of fifteen people who are Futuring on the same topic through the same exercises, the results can be very unalike in terms of the*

futures they come up with. There will be certain elements they share, but they'll have a very different flavor." - Erin

---

Should you future with your colleagues?

We recommend that only 20 to 30% of your Futurists be drawn from within your organization. These need to be the key stakeholders in your organization that we talked about before; those most closely involved with and leading on the issue or problem about which you'll be Futuring. Just as importantly, they need to have the right mindset, and the willingness to look beyond their own immediate goals and concerns. Conflict is desirable; this process is not about finding a consensus, but rather about eliciting multiple, often opposing views, and the more the better. Some ideas that come up will be at odds with current strategic objectives. *This is a good thing.* Challenge and conflict are where creativity is born, not in lockstep conformity, so your Futurists shouldn't be afraid of stepping boldly outside of the box.

WHEN WE SELECT FUTURISTS, we look for people whose backgrounds and CVs show us that they think bigger than the average person. We're looking for contrarians, disruptors, subject matter experts, strategists, collaborators, the imaginative, and end users – not always for those who hold a formal stake in the organization, although the internal champions do need to have some authority in the organization in order to be able to pull through the insights to ongoing strategic planning. And generally, outside experts bring a more matrixed view, representing all the areas needed to cover the ground we've mapped out in our landscape assessment.

That said, one of our best participants in the Pharma Beta Futuring came from inside the company, a man who had a bigger picture view of the pharma world that went beyond the perimeters of his work as an internal lead for the disease area. At Pharma Alpha, we had a similarly visionary woman who led the effort to have us Future for them, who was also asking bigger questions than those specific to her area: What will the environment for new drugs be like in ten or twenty years, and how can we use that to plan the company's actions today? Like the man at Pharma Beta, she is the kind of person that's intellectually comfortable stepping outside her role to look at the whole environment in which she's operating, so Futuring makes a lot of sense to her. For your inside stakeholders, consider – are these people who also have leadership skills, and can help to pull the results of the Futuring, as well as what they've learned in doing it, through your organizational culture?

FUTURING BRINGS another important benefit that can carry through to positive cultural change in an organization, in that it helps people pop up out of their silos like prairie dogs, and become more receptive to "seeing" the bigger picture, facilitating a more nuanced and global understanding of how the whole thing works, as well as greater potential for creative cross-pollination and problem-solving between silos. That shared ability to lift their eyes from their own objectives within the business environment to take in this bigger picture is not something day-to-day objectives always allow; as is the case for most of us, their remit is fairly narrow. However, people who Future with us report back that after Futuring, they're more likely to take it upon themselves to consider "How can I make a bigger difference?" And while Futuring doesn't free them from having to fulfill their internal mandates, they tend to bring a different perspective back with them to their everyday work, and make it relevant to what they do in their departments.

Anybody can do Futuring and come up with a whole bunch of ideas - but how you subsequently integrate it back into your mandate is really the mark of success. This is where taking the time to pause and determine how your Futuring outcome should change your future planning is vital to success. Action plans based on Futuring outcomes should be placed along a timeline with clear actions, and indications of success mapped out. If Futuring is not changing the decisions you are making *today,* then you are missing out on its greatest value.

In other words, just having imagination and vision isn't enough; there needs to be that dose of practicality, too. People who are powerfully attracted to the novelty of Futuring – the intellectual thrill ride aspect of it - and to shiny new approaches for their own sake may lack the discipline or the introspection to say, "How's this going to be relevant to our business?" They can certainly Future, but they won't necessarily have the skills needed to bring what they've learned back to help the business succeed.

AT THE OTHER end of the spectrum is the person with neither the ability nor the interest in making imaginative leaps. These people can be brilliant, with impressive CVs – but because they're so rooted in the now, they don't bring that brilliance to Futuring. One guy in particular stands out for us; Futuring for him was a waste of time, because he couldn't imagine how it would help him achieve those goals - "I don't get how that relates to me." And the fact is, the outcomes of a Futuring might not relate to you specifically, and the results may only prove themselves out years from now. But none of that is interesting to someone who's so narrowly focused on his own goals, and those kinds of people are not generally going to be helpful in a Futuring session. However, these "now-ists" can have a role during the translation of the insights from Futuring back to potential actions for the present. It's not easy, but these pragmatists can bring great value if their skills and perspectives are woven into the right place.

Why is it so important that most of the participants come from outside of your company, and even outside of your industry? While there is value to having your own people as part of the mix, when you're considering a big question that cuts across multiple disciplines, drawing your group from among the best and brightest in those areas brings the kind of diversity of insight and opinion that makes the Futuring productive and the results useful. They're not invested in the corporate mindset or in maintaining the status quo. They have no axes to grind with colleagues among you; their career paths probably don't cross your property. And their interests and insights come from a world that your world may only intersect with tangentially, if at all. Since Futuring isn't about reaching consensus, people who have very different points of view are important to the mix.

Who are my stakeholders?

Since the future could be influenced (or driven) by any one of the peripheral domains that encircle your business, the stakeholder you invite to Future with you should represent as broad an environmental context as possible. In creating your landscape assessment, you've categorized the big "buckets" that impact your issue. The next step is identifying the key stakeholders in those same buckets; the thinkers, the movers-and-shakers, researchers, academics and clinicians whose work is aligned with the areas you've identified. Again, this requires a deep dive into research on who these major influencers and thought leaders are, and a strong strategy for choosing the right ones.

In working with Pharma Beta, we looked for outside experts whose experience and points of view could cast light across the broadest possible view of the landscape in which their medication would need to be able to compete; from those who would prescribe it, those who'd pay for it, those who'd be likely to want it, etc. etc. These external stakeholders included representatives drawn from the payer world, disease specialties, digital health, Futuring, primary care, and mobile health. These individuals were chosen because their expertise was considered to be essential to any vision of the future for that particular disease area. As a rule, the disciplines considered should be as broad as possible, while keeping the number of participants manageable, as described above.

External experts to invite to your Futuring could include:

- Payers, because access and payment impact every aspect of healthcare
- Physicians, specifically those specialists who treat only this disease, because the future of disease management is going to be heavily influenced by the clinical perspective of those that know the disease the best
- Patients' representatives, because as information becomes even more accessible to patients, the role of the patient in understanding their disease and acting as their own advocate will likely increase, too
- Primary care providers, because they are the front line of defense for most diseases and they also are the provider that is most likely to 'see' the patient as a whole person
- Physicians Assistants and nurse practitioners, because they have an increasing role in the assessment and management of patients, and also tend to see the patient more holistically than does a specialist
- Nurses, because, in addition to their clinical experience, they bring a unique perspective on the patient as a person
- Radiologists, because as technology advances, it is possible that more diseases may be diagnosed on the basis of a scan or an image that may be local or remote
- Pharmacists, because they impact every aspect of care when it involves a medication or device
- Gerontologists, because we are collectively getting older, and the role of the elderly in our lives and our communities is shifting
- A.I., because the future will likely embrace AI as a tool to detect and manage disease, but also because of the

challenges with data privacy and the personalization (or depersonalization) of healthcare overall
- Digital health, because everything we do is captured somewhere
- Personalized medicine, because as we learn more about disease, the opportunities and challenges of personalized approaches will be magnified
- Public policy, because health policies have the power to limit or enhance healthy lives at scale
- Regulatory and legal, because the frameworks put in place by regulations impact how much leverage we can have with new approaches to treating disease
- Ethicists, because we are increasingly divided and the challenges of care inequity will only grow. Also, because we are more than the sum of our health and other data

BECAUSE PHARMA BETA'S focus was narrower than Pharma Alpha's, the buckets we needed to fill were fewer and less diverse than was the case with Alpha. Those chosen to participate from within Pharma Beta were drawn from senior management, who were responsible for making the budget decisions for upcoming investments.

> *"In choosing our participants, we begin with asking, "Who are people involved with this challenge right now? What does that patient pathway look like? Who are all the players involved in it? And when you're talking about an ideal future, who would you want to be in that conversation?" - Sheryl*

Because of the wider scope of their issues, Pharma Alpha's

Futuring group was drawn from a much broader spectrum of players, and included:

- Endocrinologists
- Healthcare-associated infections
- Gerontologists
- Nurses
- Health economists
- Diabetes experts
- Payers
- Digital health experts
- Public health experts
- Neurologists
- Dieticians
- Gastroenterologists
- Cardiologists
- Nephrologists
- Healthy aging experts
- Medical ethicists

As part of our preparation for Futuring with Pharma Alpha, we interviewed experts in associated fields for their insights, which became part of our landscape assessment and informed the choices we made among our experts. These interviews were with people representing expertise in the following fields:

- Pharmacy
- Genetics
- Epidemiology
- Psychology
- Ophthalmology

Also included among our participants and our interviewees were representatives, both past and present, of US and European health organizations and professional associations whose work had touched on what we were going to examine. We even brought another Futurist aboard for his insights.

> *"We looked for experts that not only aligned with the topic buckets we'd decided on, but ideally ones whose professional experience and associations allowed them to fill more than one bucket; the epidemiologist who heads a public health organization, for instance. That allows us to cover a much broader spectrum of expertise and investment with fewer participants."* - Erin

BUT DON'T MAKE the error of choosing *only* those people who are blue-sky thinkers. Here's the paradox: if you only include people who are great at Futuring and great at strategy you are going to be left with everyone saying the same kinds of things, with some differences in their spin. That's why it's a good idea to have one or two people who are in the trenches where work is getting done, from a practical perspective - linear thinkers versus strategic thinkers - because they can push you out of your comfort zone while the Futuring is in progress.

> *"Just because you're an expert in health technology doesn't mean you belong at the table. You have to be an expert in health technology who future-thinks. So, what we do is research your background and look for signs that your thinking in health technology is on the cutting edge and you have innovated or thought differently within that space."* - Erin

You've also got to be resolute about not gathering a group of people who are too much like yourself. That's harder than you might think, because we're all predisposed to prefer like-minded people who think in the same ways we do. But in putting this group together, you've got to be aware of your own prejudice and actively work to subvert it. That's why it is very useful to share the job of coming up with participants, enlisting several others in coming up with names to include on your list. Even if the people they offer aren't people whom you would necessarily have thought to include, the diversity they can potentially bring to the room is valuable for just that reason.

Whoever ends up on your list, it's always important to bring in people who have open minds. We in the healthcare field are surrounded by clinicians and scientists, and it is tempting the think that all these very smart people will naturally embrace the act of imagining the future. The truth is, though, that there are many kinds of smart and not all are suitable for Futuring.

"Sometimes we can adopt a closed mindset. We know what we know and shy away from imaginative thinking, saying, "That's never been shown, that's never been proven, it doesn't work that way, there's no evidence...". Scientists by their nature are more driven by hypotheses than mere fact. Some scientists will pretty much entertain any hypothesis. You just put it out there, and they will consider it, they will build on it and they will create a new hypothesis around it, undeterred by the lack of facts. These types of scientists tend to fail more often, but, when they succeed, our leaps in understanding of a disease or phenomenon can be great. Other scientists look to build knowledge more on facts than imagination and in doing so make ongoing and incremental increases in understanding which are also very important to the advancement of science. In my observation, 90% of scientists are the latter type; they

look for the next logical piece of the puzzle, building on what is known. These scientists form the bedrock of scientific advancement. The scientists that make the "breakthroughs" (and the people that we like to have in the room with us) are those that are willing to go beyond facts and logic, who are willing to let their imaginations run free to see what comes from it. It's a rarer kind of smart in a world full of smarts. Both types of thinking are absolutely essential to the advancement of society, of science, and to the creation of new medicines and studying disease, but those who are going to cause the paradigm shifts, the ones that are going to make the big waves, are those very, very few who have this ability to think very broadly and conceptually." - Sheryl

---

FOR TEAM MEMBERS who are tasked with choosing participants, it's best to be focused on bringing in participants whose specialties might not particularly interest you, or be in your wheelhouse of expertise. You might have a background in ophthalmology, for instance, but be assigned the job of finding a podiatrist. Since you're not involved in that area, it pushes you out of your comfort zone, helps you to look more objectively and thoroughly at candidates, and be more likely to come back with a richer description of them. As we go through this exercise, we discuss out potential attendees in depth. We justify them to each other, and if they pass muster, they get on the list. We are tough on each other; we need to be sure we have the right people, and that we can justify those choices to our client, since many of the participants will be outside of the wheelhouse of the client and their disease area.

What does all this experiential diversity bring to your Futuring? It helps combat the silos and their unfortunate tendency to block the view. A payer has some understanding of the payer market, and a patient advocate understands the patients' view, but their cross-sectional views may be fragmented. It can be as though there's a cement barrier between their respective areas of expertise, and although they may catch a glimpse of what's on the other side of it, the barrier can stop them from crossing over it or getting a high-level view. Futuring knocks down any barriers, and encourages getting out of your lane and cruising awhile in someone else's. As the walls fall away, the real scope of what you're exploring takes shape.

Identifying your experts

Once you have decided the topic areas and the types of experts you want to invite, pulling together a top-flight group of assorted authorities in multiple fields requires significant investments in both legwork and time.

The first step is identifying those leaders in the areas you need to cover. This starts with looking for names and finding *curriculum vitae* (also known as CV), an academic phrase that just means biography and work history. Any type of biography, CV or résumé will do as a start. Do they have a history of original work in the area about which you're Futuring? It's important too to try and assess how they are as collaborators – and whether they play well with others. Have they worked with teams in the past to produce important ideas? Where have they worked, and how high have they risen? Their career trajectory can give you a glimpse of how their peers and superiors have viewed their energy and value. Are they intellectually curious? The variety of work they've done and what they've published can reveal a lively and curious intellect that pushes boundaries – or a more traditional linear kind of thinking.

WHERE DO you look for your participants? The academic world is certainly a good place to start, particularly when you're Futuring on a healthcare question, because so many of the brightest and most innovative doctors and researchers are concentrated at the big universities, which usually offer both clinical and academic opportunities.

Start with the very best, the top tier in whatever discipline you're researching. We define that top tier a rather specific way: Our first choices have skills in their area of expertise, but typically they also have experience in collaborative problem solving that goes outside of their discipline. Many of them will have a forward-looking publication, or have given a lecture where they clearly show an imaginative view of their area. They may be known for their innovative approach, or for a tendency to rattle the cage of accepted orthodoxy in their field. If the top people are not available, then agree on the most desired attributes you are looking for and work your way through other potential attendees. Starting from what you consider your top candidates gives you plenty of room to backfill if necessary.

As you research and build your lists of candidates, there will likely be a significant number of people who for various reasons you can't have in the room, but whose views on your question are valuable to creating your landscape. Interviewing them is another important part of preparing to Future. While you may be confident that you understand the world in which you're Futuring without getting these people's input, you'll be surprised at what diversity of thought and ideas can come out of well-planned and thoughtfully executed interviews – and what you learn can enrich and broaden your landscape assessment.

> "Do ask those you've chosen, or those involved in outward-facing divisions within your company, who they've worked with or who they might know of that could be a good fit for the session. Then you would follow up to get in touch with a specific person– even if you've never heard of them before. We found a wonderful participant in just that way for Pharma Alpha's Futuring; someone who wasn't on our radar, but who was known by others who worked or researched in the type 2 diabetes space for her work on behalf of the aging. All roads led

to this lady; she is trying to make a global shift in how people view the older adults in the world so that they are respected and still seen as members of the community who have a lot to contribute. She very much is raising awareness of the concept that if aging adults can stay healthy, then they can continue to contribute and add value to their world. There's a huge gap between how long people live and how long they live healthy lives, and her focus is in on closing that gap between actual lives lived and healthy lives lived. Treating diabetes earlier is one of the ways you do that, so she speaks all over the place and influences very broadly. Her input was so valuable that when Sheryl was presenting the landscape assessment, we asked her to comment on what she was seeing in that sphere. She's a model choice for Futuring: she's visionary, and she's engaged in trying to change the way people think." - Erin

---

IF YOU'RE Futuring on an issue that involves public health or a specific disease or condition, foundations involved with that issue are another good place to prospect for participants. They've got the expertise and the demonstrated interest, and are likely to be on top of what's happening or about to happen in their world. Government agencies or international organizations involved in the issue are also great places to find passionate experts who know how to collaborate across their specialties – and that's important, as we'll see. We should mention there that when considering individuals from governmental organizations, it is important comply with any regulatory or compliance restrictions in working with industry.

Personality matters, too

Initial interviews will be important because you're going to be assessing more than just these peoples' expertise. As touched on earlier, personality styles play a big role in who will be valuable in the Futuring exercise, and who is likely either to try and dominate the discussion (not good) or simply withdraw from it (arguably worse). In putting together Futuring groups for clients, we employ various kinds of assessment tools to determine the likely personality types of the individuals we're talking to, because intellectual brilliance by itself isn't enough. It's not just about expertise: It's about a way of thinking and interacting.

Do they think bigger?

When you're putting together your list of expert participants, don't just look at their CVs to compare their accomplishments; look at them for hints they provide to the person's mindset. Is this person an entrepreneur? Someone with vision who's willing to take a leap of faith in pursuit of a dream? That can be a good indication that you're looking at an adventuresome thinker who'll bring a "what if...?" attitude to your Futuring. When you're interviewing them, discover if they can think outside of their space. If for instance the person is in digital health, but is in a room with people with other specialties, will they be able to make the connections between what they do and what others do?

> *"We knew going in to the Pharma Beta exercise that some people were going to be tougher than others to bring into this way of thinking, because these are the very top of their fields - super specialists who are very sure of themselves, and deservedly so, because they're saving lives every day. We bring them into an environment where we have flattened the playing*

> *field in a sense, since nobody knows the future. We are all in this together; you're a Futurist, you're a payer, you're a doctor - it doesn't really matter what your specialist area is, you are simply bringing your perspective to this future which nobody actually owns. Some are people just better at jumping into that than others."* - Sheryl

---

Are they blinkered by now-ism?

When you're interviewing, ask questions around the future; if your interviewee consistently brings the conversation back to the present, or talks about the reasons why this or that could or would never happen, this may not be the kind of broad thinker you're looking for, so that's a red flag.

Are they clearly egoists?

Does the conversation always come back to them and their accomplishments? One good way to assess whether they're overly invested in professional rivalries and feuds is to bring up other accomplished people in the suspected egoist's area of expertise; they'll almost invariably dismiss them or shoot their contributions down. Yes, big egos often come with big achievements, but when the person's ego threatens to crowd you as the interviewer out of the conversation, you can assume that they will do the same when they're Futuring.

Can they think outside of their professional box?

One woman we interviewed began her career as an engineer, but had jumped into the medical space, and eagerly described the project in which she'd been able to take her current knowledge and apply it to this entirely different and unfamiliar area with success. She sounded very attractive as a prospective Futurist; not just thinking big and having amazing crossover application ideas, but also showing willingness to learn about a whole new area outside of her specialty, in order to solve a big problem. Entrepreneurs often have this creative, free-thinking spark – the "what if...?" way of looking at things, and of problem-solving, which makes them valuable participants in Futuring.

Can they shut up and listen?

This one's pretty easy to gauge in an interview. Can the person whom you're interviewing listen without interrupting, and are they able to entertain alternate ideas or points of view without shutting you down? Do they dismiss anything that's not in their wheelhouse as not interesting to them, or as less important? Those who can't entertain or contribute ideas outside of their areas of expertise are not likely to be useful to you. Cross any interviewee off of your list if during the course of your initial phone conversation he constantly interrupts or shows signs of wanting to control the conversation. That's a hard personality type to integrate into a Futuring exercise, and you don't need someone whose inclination is to hijack the dialogue

Are they trying to sell something?

Be aware that there will be people who see your Futuring exercise as an opportunity to connect with potential clients or buyers; many people in these worlds are also paid consultants of one sort or another. Everyone comes with some sort of baggage, certainly, but they've got to be willing and able to leave those bags at the door for the day. Yes, we've seen many mutually beneficial business relationships and partnerships come out of these exercises - but prospecting can't be the primary reason they're participating. While we see the creation of those opportunities to connect as a win for all involved, and are delighted when they happen, you don't want someone coming in with a hard-sell attitude, pushing their product, because this is about you, not about them, and they have to be able to go with that agenda. We've seen unproductive situations in which people like this doggedly return to the same solutions again and again in the Futuring sessions – solutions they just happen to be selling. It's the "When you've got a hammer, every problem becomes a nail" thing, and it's not useful to your goals. When this happens, the skills of the facilitators can be sorely tested.

Are they outgoing, or introverted?

Personality type is very important; while the most obvious course might seem to be to fill the room with extroverts who can be counted on to speak up, as the facilitator, you've got to be willing to work with introverts and be skilled at drawing them out, because many of the leaders in these scientific worlds tend to introversion - and some of the best and brightest fit that personality type. One of our favorite consultants is a very quiet and introspective person, but we make a point of bringing him in and drawing out his opinion when he's in our Futuring rooms because his insights are always profoundly valuable. Yes, working with an introvert in this kind of setting will require more expert wrangling on your facilitator's part, but in our experience it's worth it, because the way the introvert processes information is often nuanced and can add a unique perspective.

"Our clients trust us to create a good balance of personalities in the room, and not to bring in anyone who's going to try and run the show. Yes, you can have those people with their personalities, but you have to accept the responsibility of managing them, and you have to create the opportunity ahead of time to allow the others to establish connections and their

own credibility – otherwise, those egos will take over. It's amazing how, if you ask the right questions, the magic will usually happen." - Erin

---

Interview etiquette

Do not waste these peoples' time; everyone you're going to be soliciting for an interview or possibly a spot in your Futuring exercise is busy, in demand and probably very judicious about where they allot their time. Make sure your interview questions are sharp, knowledgeable, and to the point. Research the person and their area of interest *before* you conduct the interview so that you can ask follow-up questions that show an understanding of their expertise and field. In other words, do your homework ahead of the call, and have an agenda.

Compensating your attendees

There is also expense to consider when you're weighing invitations to your chosen A-list. At minimum, you're going to need to pay their travel expenses and honoraria. Because these folks are at the top of their field, they may be used to getting paid a great deal more than you can afford. Those who are often called to consult or contribute may have fixed fees, so before you even begin to make these contacts, do your research on potential costs. While it may be worth it to pay outside of your usual range for certain opinions, there may be budget constraints or compliance concerns that preclude you from doing so. Understanding this aspect as soon as possible in the selection process is very important.

Turn on the bubble chart

This selection and slotting process is by its nature apt to become unwieldy because of the number and diversity of subject areas, so keeping it in order and moving forward productively requires using tools that help you see at a glance both where you are and where you need to be. We use big bubble charts for this, because they help us to visually fill in the gaps between what experts we're bringing in and what buckets they fill.

"For Pharma Alpha, we went through the bucket landscape and looked at our stakeholders; then we took our lists of potential invitees to the client to decide who we wanted to ask and who we didn't. All of the people we had for them to consider were at the tops of their respective fields. We built our bubble chart for this client starting with all of these different topic areas. Then we first put within those all of the people we wanted to interview but didn't want to invite; then, all the people we wanted to invite but not interview - creating a sort of big map that helped to inform our landscape view. With our interviews, we did what nearly amounted to a mini-Futuring that helped us gather qualitative research that helped us in preparing the quantitative research of the landscape we were preparing. We created a series of questions; for instance, what did these people see as the most important innovations in medicine in the past five years?" - Kelly

"The balance matters, when you're preparing both the qualitative and quantitative research: There needs to be a good mesh between the hard data, which is quantitative and includes all the references we've found, with the more perspective-driven, more subjective data we're getting from our interviewees – what we call the soft data." – Sheryl

OUR BEST ADVICE on how to get the most out of your pre-Futuring preparation step? *Don't skimp.* Even though you might think that it is obvious what topic areas you need to cover, *do* brainstorm with your colleagues to see what you might be missing. You need to come up with the broadest possible spectrum of experts and organizations. Start with online search engines to begin assembling lists of potential invitees, and to review their press, their publications, and their professional associations. Then do the brainstorming to fill in the gaps, and create organizational charts to help you keep track of who you're looking at and what boxes they check.

"An advantage for us as facilitators in preparing these lists of potential participants is that we've got a growing bench of world-class experts with whom we've worked all across the healthcare professional spectrum, and with whom we've successfully Futured. Many of these are people we call on to join in multiple exercises, both for their extensive knowledge and for their ability to look creatively at the future. It's great to work with them, because they're big-picture thinkers who are comfortable with both being challenged on their ideas and with challenging others. They know our process, they know how we work, and they can support that; they have a really good perspective and they are at the top of their respective fields." - Kelly

---

Create both an A and B list of potential guests for each category you intend to fill; also, create a list of those who you'll want to interview, but who you will not invite to your Futuring. Make sure your budget can accommodate paying these people and their expenses, as well as expenses for the site of the Futuring itself. In our opinion, it's better to future off-site and away from your company Futurists' workaday environment because they're less likely to feel the pull to "check in", so include the costs of a venue in your budget planning. You'll also need to include the costs associated with setting the stage – which we'll discuss in detail further on.

Key Points for Chapter 6

1. Decide how many of your colleagues to invite.
2. Define your stakeholders and all the threads you need to touch.
3. Skill, experience and level of influence matter.
4. Personality matters too; it can make or break a session.
5. Turn the bubble chart full on!

SEVEN

MAPPING YOUR WORLD

A significant preparation step for Futuring is creating a world view of the now.

On the day of the Futuring, all Futurists will gather in the main room for introductions and a review of the current landscape. This provides an overview of the key topic areas represented by the experts in the room and suggests some of the current trends that may or may not impact the future of healthcare. The landscape view can be a relatively short presentation, giving the current trends at a high level, vs a deep dive. A Powerpoint presentation works well, although a video that shows current healthcare challenges can also be used. We want to make the audience think outside of their expertise by giving them a flavor of the big picture they will be Futuring later in the day. All of the research, including interviews with non-participating experts, will be included in the landscape presented. Think about the key questions you really want answered.

These are question such as:

- What are the current challenges in healthcare as a whole?

- How is the US healthcare system doing, compared to others in rich, developed nations? (The Commonwealth fund is a great resource for this.)
- In my areas of interest, what is the public talking about, on both the positive side and the negative?
- What are scientists talking about?
- What are the recent developments in the field?
- What is being reported in the media?
- What is appearing in the literature?
- What are the major trends in my top areas?
- What are the controversies and agreements appearing today?

A typical landscape will include high-level trends from several sources:

- *The people you have interviewed:* This content will be subjective so it is important to indicated it as such. By keeping the questions consistent from interview to inter.view, you will be better able to extract the trends in perception around the key issues. The interview data is usually presented as the questions we asked and a summary statement or two based on the responses you get.
- *The scientific literature:* This landscape research takes some time. It will involve retrieving recent reviews of the field as well as recent study outcomes, and getting a sense of the recent discoveries and the most pressing challenges that have still to be solved. The intent is to show the current questions experts are wrestling with and the progress towards answers.
- *Internet searching including news and social media:* Searching the web with keywords that match to the areas of interest will net a significant about of data in multiple

contexts. You should look for media/news reports to see what is being reported. Look at social media for what patients and physicians are talking about. Check regulatory websites for latest drug approvals and recent controversies in medical treatment. Look up press releases and conferences to see what experts are lecturing on, and what the top guys are being asked about.
- *Consider mapping institutions and key individuals*: It's not always necessary for Futuring, but definitely necessary for the next steps.

Typically, there are six to seven main topic areas chosen for the landscape. As an example, the following is a set of topics for a hypothetical Futuring around the future of adult influenza vaccines:

- Vaccine regulations
- Healthy living environments
- Health disparities and access challenges
- Healthcare delivery trends
- Scientific understanding (of immunity, vaccines, infection trends, vaccine production, etc.)
- Social determinants of elder health

You can choose whatever topics best suit your Futuring area, but limit them to fewer than ten if possible, so the presentation to the Futuring attendees doesn't get too complicated. As you extract the insights for your research, don't be afraid to call out controversies. There are several areas that are agnostic to the disease you are interested in. For instance, there are startling statistics on how much healthcare costs in the US, relative to the outcomes we achieve. Placed alongside other wealthy nations, the US does poorly in this cost/outcome ratio. Regardless of your main topic to disease area, if you live and work in the US, this is of great interest, both in the now, and for the potential future. Similarly, digital health challenges are universal, and will impact every version of the healthcare future no matter what part of the system you are working in.

You'll want your presentation to be as broad as possible; all the expertise you can pull together, all pertinent numbers you can crunch, all the expert views you can summarize, digest and present as high-level trends, and what they mean to the future. This part matters because people need to go into the exercise primed with the same basic understanding of where we are today, regardless of the discipline they represent.

An important dimension of data we include in Futuring is social data, which we gather by going on social sites and listening to what people are saying on the topic on which we're Futuring. These conversations might happen on patient advocacy sites, for instance, or even on Facebook, where people create groups to share their thoughts around an issue, or to swap information about treatment, new medications, warnings, etc. This information can be quite valuable in preparing the landscape, because what the quantitative data show us – for instance, a study that talks about what the impact of a disease has been on a population over the last ten years – may be contradicted in the social strata, because people simply don't believe or accept that study as fact, creating a disconnect of which our Futurists need to be aware. We also include the potential impact of artificial intelligence to change the ways we share and react to social data. Big data is finally beginning to deliver insight into how symptoms cluster for instance. For our diabetes challenge with Pharma Alpha, big data was a very hot topic, because of the potential to develop algorithms for risk and health outcomes for a disease that most certainly has not only symptom clusters but also biomarker clusters and genotypic clusters.

Those disconnects are increasingly common now that social media has taken the place of other kinds of research or doctor/patient conversations for many. As we've noted in earlier chapters, the individual's perspective and beliefs are increasingly important in a world where it seems that facts are irrelevant or discounted. Beliefs have always been an important factor in decision-making, but the power of shared beliefs has gotten a tremendous boost as social media have provided platforms for the exchange of these ideas and the bringing together of those who share a special interest. Often, especially in healthcare and medicine, we see that the gap between what we know to be fact and what people who are more personally concerned with the issue believe is true, can be huge.

A good example of that would be the rise of the anti-vaxxer platform, which could never have occurred (at least not to the extent that it has) had the Internet not existed. That matters, and needs to be addressed because if your Futuring problem necessitates reaching people and convincing them to act in a particular way, you need to know how to speak to their beliefs. That will impact how you shape your decisions, and how you might create your messaging down the road.

All of these kinds of research and background work are very useful to companies, because it allows them to connect the dots in a way they do not necessarily get to do in their day to day operations. Bringing this information "across the hall" provides a new perspective and a clearer view of what perceptions are in play in the worlds of knowledge and belief.

> *"Working with Pharma Beta, we were able to put together a really comprehensive landscape presentation that got the Futurists excited about the exercise; some of the quotes we got from physicians we interviewed stimulated lively discussions and worthwhile conversations. I think our way of Futuring, even though it's relatively brief, can be quite comprehensive. We bring all of these elements in, in a very focused way, right to this landscape analysis. The presentation we give as a result, is high level but very concise which I think is a strength of our approach."* - Sheryl

One of the most valuable parts of pulling together and reviewing the landscape at the start of the exercise is that everyone starts to make connections and see things from a fresh perspective. It's a great precursor to the actual Futuring. The energy in the room amps up when you start to dig into that landscape. It whets the Futurists' appetites for what's to come, and gets them into that blue-sky, wide-open frame of mind. There are often disagreements of the insights we present which, again, are a good way to warm up the crowd for the Futuring ahead.

"Another great benefit that comes after Futuring is the team-building it creates within the organization, and the inspiration it brings. While you discourage group-think before and during the Futuring, once you have your outcomes, you need to create a common purpose that didn't exist before, that rallies people together across their silos to bring about this vision. It really makes for a more highly-functional and cohesive organization." - Erin

Landscapes can create alliances

An important aspect for Pharma Alpha in building their landscape was connecting all of these institutions that had an interest in the problem they were Futuring on, but who weren't necessarily in communication with each other before we put them in touch. Part of our research in looking for who the central people are in these institutions and finding out who's doing what, and who's driving it. We created a map of all the stakeholders from an institutional perspective who were involved in diabetes. We had people who had previously worked at the CDC, WHO, as well as private companies and academic institutions; we had a European technical group that funded research and had created a whole project around the topic; we found a private group in the UK who were also funding research; and these were all connected either through a grant or through a specific person, so we were able to classify them as being private, academic, or a mix, and then also identify who were some of the key linkages between them.

We provided Pharma Alpha with a comprehensive partner map, so that when they had gone through their Futuring and came out the other end saying, "We need to do x, y, and z", they were able to look at the map and see who they might partner with to help them accomplish those outcomes. This map listed all the institutional players, along with their connections, and provided tremendous value in implementation. And, as a result of creating that map, we were able to invite some of those people who were involved in some of these initiatives, so we already had the right people in the room with whom they could potentially join to take the next steps. That created a huge and valuable edge for a project with large potential implications across multiple companies and multiple sectors.

WITH SMALLER COMPANIES, or companies Futuring on a more narrowly focused question, the map is still very useful; just less complex and densely populated. In both cases, the map enables and inspires new synergy, new partnerships, and fruitful working alliances.

"We saw that in action at Pharma Beta, who were interested in exploring digital health as a way to collect data on the condition that their medication treats. Data mining was an option, but where were the repositories of that data? One of the experts we brought in spoke up, saying that he was doing a project on that topic, and was collecting information that would be useful to Pharma Beta. They're working together now, sharing information, from an opportunity they would

probably never have known existed had they not been Futuring with the people in that room. Even for a smaller company, doing some of that mapping upfront to get the right people in the room added a lot of value, though theirs was a much more narrowly targeted project than was Pharma Alpha's." - Kelly

---

In the example below, you'll see the big topics/high points we introduced to the groups from Pharma Alpha's landscape assessment – what the current state of type 2 diabetes looks like:

Landscape Assessment for Pharma Alpha:

- Diabetes research is very active, and the scientific understanding of it as a multi-system disease is growing
- Significant learnings from successful new diabetes drugs
- We struggle to achieve diagnosis and treatment goals for adults
- Delivery of diabetes treatment is inconsistent
- Access to new diabetes products is unreliable
- Public apathy to diabetes sets back progress for the disease and its consequences
- There is indifference to diabetes from some treating in the community
- Patients under-appreciate personal disease risk
- Affordability is a barrier across the globe
- Implementation is hampered by ineffective partnerships across sectors

---

"For Pharma Alpha, this overview covered the patient view, the payer's view, diabetes, healthcare in the world and the US, and

chronic health problems for the aging. We dug into challenges presented by the healthcare systems here and abroad." - Sheryl

Statistics and charts helped the listeners understand the scope of the challenge and who the stakeholders were.

"The landscape that I normally present takes a half hour to an hour at most: it's really to set the scene across all of the areas that might impact the problem. What the landscape overview is supposed to do is to take all the different disciplines that we are going to be integrating into our Futuring discussion and just say here is a snapshot of where we are in the world in the payer landscape or the healthcare environment in general that we think is relevant and important. Someone is inevitably going to say "Well, that's not inclusive" or "But you didn't talk about this or that". The fact is, it's not intended to be all-inclusive; it's intended to set a scene for where we are in the overall landscape and you cannot possibly be fully inclusive on everything." - Sheryl

"It's a very high level snapshot in time, because if we tried to cover it all in detail we'd be in trouble. What it accomplishes beyond that – and what we saw a lot of during the Pharma Alpha Futuring exercise – was that it sparked conversations between people from different areas and led to some interesting partnerships that cut across these disciplines, because when we got all these people together from all these different areas it was the only time they had all been in the same place. There was a real sense of potential; of people saying, "I think this is a problem, too, and even though you and I are coming at it from

totally different directions, with all of our brains together, we can do something cool."' - Erin

---

Key points for Chapter 7

1. Presenting a high-level landscape view gives your Futurists a shared picture of where you are now.
2. This landscape will include information you've gleaned in your research from multiple sources, including interviews with experts, scientific literature, internet searches and social media, and mapping of key institutions and individuals involved in the area on which you're Futuring.
3. Choose more than five but fewer than ten main topics for your landscape.
4. Keep it high-level; set the scene but don't get bogged down in minutia. The goal is to tell the story of the now, to level set, and provide topic areas that will inform the discussion in the Futuring sessions.

EIGHT
THE NIGHT BEFORE FUTURING

Creating a unique environment in which to place your Future is a key piece of preparation. How imaginatively you approach this stage-setting determines how easily your Futurists will be able to make the visionary jump required when you begin the actual Futuring. It's stagecraft, and you need to approach it in that way; as an immersive sensory experience.

OUR PRE-FUTURING SCHEDULE begins the night before the day of the exercise, and ends with a follow up meeting to discuss insights and potential impacts to the present day. Sometimes that follow-up meeting happens the day after the actual Futuring -but it can be weeks after the Futuring session has been completed.

Gathering everyone together on the night before Futuring gives people time to get to know each other, and is important because they are typically so diverse. A group dinner the night before allows time to break the ice, which means everyone's full attention can be on Futuring the next day.

If the follow-up is to take place immediately after the Futuring session, then we schedule a night in which Futurists can decompress, before everyone gathers to talk about what we've learned and the conclusions we can draw from it.

This is an important part of the process, because while it may sound like an easy day, Futuring is actually exhausting, albeit in a cerebral way. Trying to pack too much into one day leaves people drained, and diminishes the quality and quantity of the feedback. Giving them that extra night to rest and consider what they've talked about makes for a much more meaningful and productive final session.

Breaking the ice

The first choice you have to make is how to get all of these disparate and mostly unacquainted people into a room together and talking, ahead of beginning the Futuring process. You want them to break the ice and to begin to connect. In our experience, the most productive Futuring sessions follow a convivial, no-stress evening built around a theme; one that can lead to easy conversation that has nothing to do with the topic you'll be Futuring on. That's important, because you don't want your people to get into the topic until you've properly introduced it and set up the ground rules.

In gathering our international cast of experts together for their first encounter for one of our clients, we planned a dinner party based on the concepts of healthy eating, as presented in the series of books written about the common threads in the world's longest-lived communities, *The Blue Zones* by Dan Buettner. As it happened, few of the Futurists knew each other or were more than passingly aware of the Blue Zone research that had hinted at the secrets of longevity, so immediately everyone was put on the same neophyte level. There were cards at each of the dining tables, explaining what we'd be eating and how the menu choices fit into the Blue Zones. The concept sparked curiosity and interest; it got our group talking and they started to get to know each other around a concept that none of them was expert in, which was exactly what we'd intended.

On one occasion one of our invited guests had come in with a pretty negative attitude to the whole Futuring idea, well beyond skepticism to outright contempt. But once he sat down at his table and began interacting with experts in fields other than his, he began to see the value in hearing these disparate and unusual points of view, and to be excited about participating and learning more from these people. We could literally see the ice melt!

Like any of us, highly successful people can be competitive and hierarchical in their worldview. For some, it's part of why they're high achievers. While that sort of jockeying for position arguably has value in building a career, in Futuring it's something you want to curb as efficiently as possible, and early on. Experts know they're experts, and while most people are interested in and open to hobnobbing with their fellow wizards, not all of them are willing to share their spot in the pecking order – or what they see as their spot.

We have found an effective way to short-circuit this kneejerk response; by providing each of the guests with the professional profiles of all the people we've gathered together, so that they can begin to understand and value the others' expertise before they began Futuring together. Everyone there is an expert; everyone is a leader in his or her field, so it is important to choose a topic that is of human interest but that no attendee is a considered expert in. That stimulates interest in each other without stepping on anyone's toes, and fosters mutual respect.

SOMETHING LIKE A BLUE Zone dinner is just one way to accomplish the task of creating a more relaxed and collegial atmosphere. The key is flattening the playing field, because once the egos are curbed, each player realizes he or she isn't the only brilliant mind in the room, barriers begin to fall and people connect in a more positive and genuine way as they recognize each other's humanity. The experience is both humbling, and freeing.

What made the Blue Zone interesting as a theme was that in this Futuring we were dealing with type 2 diabetes and the Blue Zone is about healthy aging; it explores nine principles - what they call the Power Nine - that are common across society in these communities with a relatively high number of centenarians, so it tied into this general idea of taking control of your diet and health as you get older, without explicitly mentioning diabetes.

On another occasion, when a client was Futuring about respiratory medicine, we researched all the foods that help improve respiratory health, and built a dinner menu around those. Since the relationship between food and lung health is not well-understood from a scientific perspective, our approach was also not overly scientific. It was intended to stimulate a new kind of conversation, not debate the science behind the observations. Again, it got the strangers we'd gathered at the table talking to each other and thinking about ideas that weren't necessarily ones they dealt with every day.

There are plenty of other kinds of menus, venues, and possibilities for this initial social meeting, so get imaginative. It doesn't have to be a dinner, although we find that a sit-down dinner basically forces all the attendees to interact for a decent period of time, in a way that a buffet or cocktail party (where everyone's moving around the room, just dipping a toe into brief conversations) really do not. It's by its nature convivial and invites relaxed conversation and story sharing. We toyed with the idea of holding the pre-meeting dinner at an oxygen bar. Logistics prevented us from following through on the idea, but don't be afraid to explore something out of the box.

WE DO NOT SUGGEST DOING an activity that creates a competitive atmosphere, like laser tag or a locked room-type mystery game, because that will draw out the very competitiveness that you are trying to avoid. It's not the kind of interrelationship you want to foster for the Futuring session.

Stay away from the typical team-building kinds of exercises: Remember, you're not trying to team-build. On the contrary, the success of your Futuring exercise counts on people remaining independent thinkers, not on building any kind of consensus.

"Group-think is the enemy of productive Futuring. Your Futurists are there to offer contrasting, differing ideas, not create a homogeneous consensus." - Erin

---

Setting your scene

How do you design that ideal stage set – one that will get the imaginative juices flowing, and take your people far out of their workaday worlds? Simply put, surprise them. We find that having two arrestingly different and uniquely-decorated rooms in which to Future helps to push your Futurists out of their comfort zones immediately on entering. Depending on where you stage this – and we've done these exercises in several kinds of venues – you're going to have more or less leeway in terms of what's feasible or practical – but do not be tempted to skimp on this piece of preparation, because if you do it right, the sudden shift in environment it creates when they enter that unfamiliar and surprising room jolts your Futurists just enough to make them ultra-aware and more responsive – which is exactly what you want.

In our Futurings, we set about creating a "light" room and a "dark" room, because we want our people to jump right into a positive and a negative future – and an immersive environment creates the mood to get that ball rolling. We can even set up something that looks like a future venue for stakeholders; a room set up like a New Age hospital or doctor's office can work extremely well.

Our light room is cheerful and ideally has an outside view; sun streams in at the windows (weather allowing) and the lighting is pleasant and bright. Lamps are bright, with bulbs that are warm in color. The furniture is comfortable, and upholstered in light, bright colors. The air may be scented with something that smells clean and bright – a light citrus scent, for instance. The facilitator (in the bright room, it's always Sheryl) wears a light-colored and cheerful ensemble, and the whole atmosphere of this, the light room, is curated to make the people entering it feel happy and upbeat.

The dark room is very different. Any sunlight from the windows is muffled by heavy, light-blocking drapes. Lamps are either low or off altogether. The furniture is dark and unwelcoming; the chairs are spartan and may even be a little uncomfortable. The air is scented in this room too, but not pleasantly: We aim for something musty, dank, and vaguely unsettling. Don't overdo it, though! In either room, the smells can become overpowering by the end of the meeting. The scents in both rooms should be kept very subtle. Consider using a diffuser, but with just one or two sticks inserted to keep the fragrance intensity to a minimum. Erin always hosts this room wearing funereal black, and leads her group in thinking about a dark future. We've actually had people coming from the light room stop in the doorway as they entered the dark room – and backpedal right out of there! That's a testament to how effective this stage setting is at creating the mood.

"Sheryl always presides over the light room, and I'm always in the dark room, wearing a black dress. Someone once asked me as they came in, "Are you the Grim Reaper?" I took it as a compliment." - Erin

"Erin's so good at hosting the dark future that some of our

Futurists actually find it hard to shake off the feelings it leaves them with, to come into my bright future!" - Sheryl

---

Key points for Chapter 8

1. Arrange an event the night before Futuring so that your people can get to know each other before they Future together the following day.
2. Choose a theme for the event that is related to your area of interest, but keep it high-level so nobody is compelled to be a "expert" during the experience.
3. If you choose a dinner as your event, use the theme to create novelty in the food items on the menu that will in itself will get the attendees talking to each other.
4. Do not use team-building tactics at the pre-meeting dinner. Similarly, do not introduce any activities that may make the attendees feel competitive towards one another.
5. Set up the rooms for the next day. Make one light and airy for the positive future; the other dark and somewhat oppressive for the negative future. Use smells to enhance the atmosphere - but don't overdo it!

NINE
THE FUTURE IS NOW

Every Futurist has his or her own recipe for how to run a Futuring. What they include has a lot to do with the scope of the question under consideration and even more so, the length of the sessions themselves. If you've got an in-house Futuring arm, or if you're committed to doing a week-long exercise, your options are more expansive. Obviously in a more compact exercise, there has to be some perimeters set and a common understanding of what will happen once the Futuring begins. What do we hope to reap from this exercise, and how do we quantify a successful Futuring? We have found that the clearer people are going in, the more productive these Speed Futuring sessions are.

As we prepare to go into the Futuring exercise, the general directives/big goals presented to the whole group at this point will be something like these:

- Explore alternative futures (desired and undesired) for healthcare and the potential impacts to your disease area
- Determine the attributes of the future

- Explore the drivers-- what had to happen for this future to exist
- Discussion of the implications for the company and its product/offering
- Identify key value levers, and develop actionable recommendations that can support your efforts to help shape the future

Drawing the perimeters

While each of the two rooms – the dark and the light – has its own very specific identity, you'll see that the goals for what we want to accomplish in each of them are structured similarly, albeit as mirror images of each other. Again, the aim here isn't to stifle imaginative extemporizing as much as it is to keep everyone on task, on schedule, and moving deliberately toward the stated goals.

IN THE LIGHT ROOM / *The Desirable Future*

Goal: to identify the features of a desirable future healthcare environment, where the management of the disease fits in this future, the impact of this future on the disease, and to brainstorm how the client might lead the way to this idealized future.

Outputs:

- Key attributes and drivers
- Implications for the treatment of interest
- Top 3 most desired outcomes
- Ideas regarding the client's ability to shape this future in the next 3–5 years (up to 3 ideas)

Framing questions:

- What is it?

- We ask our Futurists to close their eyes and imagine what the desirable future looks like. How does it feel to be there?
- How does the healthcare world look in this future?
- How are patients impacted?
- How does living in this future impact their work and how they feel about it?
- Use the bubble chart to prompt thinking in particular areas if necessary
- How did we get here?
- What are the key drivers that helped create it?
- What had to happen for this future to become a reality?
- Which of these could be viewed at the global level, and which would be local?
- What does it mean for us?
- What are the implications in this future for your disease area?
- What is the most aspirational outcome we can imagine?
- What are the 2–3 most desired outcomes in this scenario? What would facilitate these outcomes from a global perspective?
- What are 2–3 areas where the client can engage with an activity or partnership to have the greatest impact relative to your disease are in this future, and what can we do in the next 3–5 years?

IN THE DARK ROOM/ *The Undesirable Future*

Goal: to identify the features of an undesirable future healthcare environment, the impact of this future of the disease, and postulate how the client might position itself to help avoid that future or be insulated from its effects.

Outputs:

- Key attributes and drivers
- Implications for treatment for treatment of interest
- Top 3 most feared outcomes in this scenario
- Ideas regarding the client's potential to avoid this future in the next 3–5 years (up to 3 ideas)

Framing questions:

- What is it?
- We ask the Futurists to close their eyes and begin by considering what this undesirable future looks and feel like.
- How is it impacting the world of healthcare?
- How is it impacting patients?
- How has it changed how they work, and how they feel about the work they do?
- Use the bubble chart to prompt thinking in particular areas if necessary
- How did we get there?
- What are the key drivers that helped create it? Which of these could be viewed at the global level?
- What were the key events, or developments, that had to happen for this future to come to pass?
- What does it mean for us?
- What are the implications in this future for your disease area?
- What is the worst that can happen?
- What are the 2–3 most feared outcomes in this scenario?
- What would facilitate avoidance or mitigation of these outcomes from a global perspective?
- What are 2–3 areas where the client could engage with an activity or partnership to have the greatest impact relative to the disease area and related treatments in this future, and what can we do in the next 3–5 years?

- Ideas regarding the client's potential to avoid this future in the next 3–5 years (up to 3 ideas)

Every Futuring session is different, but for the client, the day went as follows: After the presentation of the landscape assessment and before the actual Futurings began, we took a few minutes to lay down the ground rules for our Futurists when they were inside and outside of the dark and light rooms. We made it clear that the facilitators were in charge, and if they indicated it was time to move onto a new discussion, everyone needed to roll with that. It's hard in the heat of a lively discussion to let a particularly fruitful or interesting (to you) topic go – but again, time management matters, someone's got to do it, and that someone is the facilitator.

In addition to reminders about the delicate balance between allowing the full expression of the Futurists' imaginations, versus not straying off too far off topic or running out the clock, we suggested that during meals and breaks, people take the time to talk to each other; that in the meetings they make a point to both listen and to contribute, and that they allowed others to do the same.

THROUGH EXPERIENCE, we've discovered that it's critical that our futurists have dedicated spaces and time set aside in the agenda, for decompression between sessions. It allows for some breathing room, and a place to chat to others as people make the mental and emotional shift from one future to the next. We encourage them to use the space to breathe and shake off the future they've just experienced, and to get ready for the next experience.

Since these sessions are scheduled to last no longer than 90 minutes per room, the facilitator has to keep the conversation on point, because it's easy to get excited about a particular topic, and people who are involved in a discussion quickly lose track of time. That's why the facilitator has to run Futurings with both ears open and one eye on the clock. Part of what makes this Speed Futuring work so well are those time constraints; they bring a sense of urgency and purpose to the discussion, and keep everyone on task.

As facilitators we make sure that external Futurists lead discussions; it's easy for internal stakeholders to dominate the conversation, both because they have very specific ideas around the topic and because they tend to have a sense of ownership about the proceedings. While it's indisputable that they're the hosts, it's better for the outcomes if they talk a little less and listen a little more.

Into the future

Half of your people will be going into the light room first, while the other half will begin their Futuring experience in the dark room. Apart from the very different settings and moods of the respective rooms, the way in which the Futuring proceeds at this point are otherwise largely the same.

We give our Futurists a moment to get settled in their chairs, to take in the atmosphere we've curated for them, and then we ask them to sit quietly, with their eyes closed, and imagine they are in the respective future for the room.

For a few minutes, nobody speaks – then the dark future facilitator, Erin, (or Sheryl in the light room) asks everyone to offer some words that describe how they feel about the future in which they have imagined themselves to be. The Futurists are asked, "How do you feel? How do you feel about what you do? What is your experience as a patient?" We go around the room, jotting down key words in the responses on a white board.

During the Pharma Beta exercise, the answers in the light room were along the lines of:

- I'm so *happy* to go to work as a physician
- As a patient, I feel *well cared for and safe*
- I'm *proud* of the work we accomplish
- I feel *optimistic and rejuvenated*

- I feel *engaged and secure*
- I feel *appreciated and respected*

In the dark room, people are feeling very differently; the words we were getting around the dark health care future were:

I feel...

- ...*frustrated*
- ...*frightened*
- ...*fragmented*
- ...*disappointed*
- ...*hopeless*
- ...*helpless*
- ...*unimportant*
- ...*isolated*
- ...*controlled*

We then turn to the white wall, which is a literally a strip of white paper that goes the length of the room. This is our brainstorm area and the place we will construct our healthcare future. Now that we know how our Futurists feel, we want them to come up with some attributes of this healthcare state they are in.

In the dark future for Pharma Beta, some of the attributes we heard were:

- People can't get the care they need
- Frustration among patients and caregivers alike is rife
- There are too few doctors available, and in many cases none nearby
- Hospitals are closing, and those that are left are overcrowded
- Vital care isn't always available
- Patients experience long waits for care, especially for operations

In the cheerful room of the bright future, Sheryl paints a picture of a world of optimal healthcare:

- Access is good for the treatment and medications you need.
- You don't have to worry about where you'll get your healthcare – it will be there for you.
- Doctors are valued and are freed to spend their office visit time with their patients, not hanging over laptops, entering data.
- Healthcare is free for everyone, and readily available. There are no health disparities.

"It's like we're offering them a fruit bowl, and asking them to select from it. In my room, if you like cherries, it's full of gorgeous cherries. In Erin's room, they're overripe and flyblown – or the bowl's full of stones." - Sheryl

---

Digging a little deeper, we asked what the reasons were behind the bleak view.

In Pharma Beta's dark room, people told us...

- Costs for healthcare are out of sight – only the rich can afford it.
- There's no provision for the poor, or very little. Wait times are long, and people die waiting for needed care.
- Medicines are too expensive for most people to afford.
- All the best doctors have left the country, and there are too few left to manage the patients they have.
- Providers retire early from medicine because it's all paperwork and forms.

- Medicine is increasingly dumbed down to an algorithm, and anyone can do it (though not well).
- Medical providers are less well-trained, less knowledgeable, and can't reliably diagnose anything without internet access.
- The government has instituted mandatory euthanasia for the aged and the chronically ill, because they're using up too much of our limited healthcare resources.

Those in the light room were seeing a very different system. In the bright future:

- Doctors are respected and they can override the "system" if their opinion differs from what the computer says.
- You can consult every expert in the world with a few keystrokes, and have access to a vast knowledge base.
- High quality healthcare is free or nearly so, and available to all.
- Everyone can get the medications they need.
- People enjoy good health for much longer in life, and healthy aging is the norm.

With the right setting and preparation, we can get into the future very quickly and can elicit deeply personal responses from people who've been in their respective room for only about five minutes. This is typical of how well Speed Futuring can work, in terms of quickly engaging your Futurists.

As facilitators, we balance probing more deeply into the questions at hand with letting the conversation take its natural course, and not breaking the flow or focus of the future scenario.

Questions we asked in both the light and dark groups in the Pharma Alpha exercise drilled down on topics to create an understanding of what had to happen for the particular future to exist. Briefly, the questions were framed something like this:

- What has happened to make medicines more - or less - accessible to the patient?
- What is the patient's journey to a treatment for type 2 diabetes? How many opportunities exist to treat high blood sugar in an adult? Who can administer the drug since it will not be oral?
- Who are the drivers of the diabetes and metabolic health culture?
- Are medical societies engaged with pharma in this scenario?
- What are the opportunities for mobile heath in education, tracking, data gathering, etc.?
- Who are the primary stakeholders advocating on behalf of type 2 diabetes?

Once we have all the attributes on the white wall, and we have identified the underlying drivers, we start to gather opinions on the more feared or desired aspects of the futures respectively.

We also ask for ideas regarding Pharma Alpha's potential to either steer toward the bright future in the next three to five years, or away from the dark future in that time frame. After ensuring we have covered all bubbles in our topic wheel, we wrap up the session and prepare to move to the other future.

AT THE END of each session the facilitator chooses a group scribe; someone who will be responsible for summarizing the ideas and suggestions that came out of their group for all Futurists, when the exercises are done. While as facilitators we're busy writing up the big ideas on our wall boards as people are talking, the scribe's job is essential since they will be tasked with presenting those views and ideas from the Futurists' point of view.

After each 90-minute Futuring, the Futurists move into a brief decompression period before the next Futuring group session begins.

How to choose the group scribe

How do you choose someone to summarize the big ideas from among your Futurists? First, we'd suggest that the person you choose be someone who was active and engaged in the discussion, not somebody who was passive and didn't really engage. Did they have ideas, and were they good at sharing them? They also need to be able to fairly and fully represent ideas that aren't necessarily their own. That's important because people can very easily represent their ideas back to the group - but the scribe's job requires them to properly represent the ideas of the group. A group scribe has to be able to be very balanced in the way they present ideas back and also be willing to engage their team, who are invited to jump in to clarify or add to the presentation as it's made.

"The people who are naturally going to be good at this become evident to you as facilitator as you are going through the session. Occasionally, you hit a session in which nobody seems to fit that mold. That did happen to me once, actually with Pharma Alpha, when we were in a Futuring session; I asked one guy, "Can you present back?" because he had been very vocal and because, frankly, nobody else wanted to do it. Initially he refused, but I talked him into it; "You really are the best person for the job; you had the best ideas, you were highly engaged through the whole thing, you grasped what everyone was saying – you're the natural choice". He reluctantly agreed to do it, but I had to prep him for it during the decompression period and over lunch because he didn't feel comfortable doing it unless everything was laid out. We made him a chart for reference. Once he got up there, he was terrific. Some people are okay with winging it, but he wasn't. He did a terrific job." - Erin

---

The decompression process

As we've noted elsewhere, when your people have finished Futuring in their first "room", and regardless which room they began with, it's imperative that you provide an opportunity for them to decompress and "come down" from the experience they've just had. If you're tempted to leave this step out because you judge it as unimportant, *please don't*. It's critical to your success.

First of all, Futuring is exhausting, and rushing people from one experience into a completely opposite one means you're not going to get the same quality of response from them as you did in the first room. Another reason to create space and time for your people to decompress between rooms is that, once they've spent time in one room, it influences the way in which they're going to respond to the second room. Whether that's going from light to dark, or from dark to light, the first experience will color how they react to the second. That's particularly true with more sensitive, imaginative and thoughtful people.

In a way, for those coming from the light room, the dark room will be just a little less dark than it was for those who started their day there. For those transitioning out of the dark room, it's difficult to shake off the pessimism and sense of helplessness that environment creates. Your dark place is a little less dark and your bright place is a little less bright. The decompression zone is a neutralization room, where they can dial down to zero again.

How can you facilitate that decompression? Give your Futurists something simple and relatively mindless to do; a few minutes playing a game like UNO, a small puzzle to do; even a game of Trivia or 20 Questions -anything that will take them out emotionally of the Futuring space they've just been in, for twenty minutes or a half hour. You can also just let them check their phones and go to the bathroom, but we've found that leaving them without something to focus on doesn't really accomplish the goal of decompression. A special place to sit and take a pause can also work. A few minutes of guided meditation can be extremely helpful, but you must let everyone check their phones first, because otherwise nobody can concentrate! Alternately you can use a similar place to solve a few puzzles. Word games and tactile puzzles can be placed at a few stations in the decompression space and attendees can work their way around the stations, completing the puzzles.

FUTURING ISN'T JUST DEMANDING for the people doing it, of course; it's tough to facilitate, too, and the emotions Futuring stirs up can lead to all kinds of surprising reactions. In the next chapter we'll talk about some of the more common issues you'll face as a facilitator, as well as those out-of-left-field reactions that can take you by surprise.

Key points for Chapter 9

1. Create a list of framing questions to help guide your Futurists' discussion.
2. Sessions should last no longer than 90 minutes each for the Dark and Light rooms.
3. Use bubble charts as prompts to discussion if necessary.
4. Appoint a group scribe to take down Futurists' ideas for summarizing afterwards.
5. Create a space and make time for your Futurists to decompress between their time in the light and the dark rooms.

TEN

CHALLENGES FOR THE FACILITATOR

Futuring can be an unexpectedly emotional experience for people, especially the dark future: Sometimes we find that a highly sensitive person will really be shaken by the dark room experience. One woman, Susan, who was part of the Pharma Beta group, simply could not leave the light room behind, emotionally. Susan had been fine in the light room, but once she was in the dark room and we'd gone through the stage-setting talk, her response was literally, "I don't want to be here; this is horrible. I hate this place that you've brought me to"- and she started texting on her phone.

Erin tried to draw her out - "Susan, what would happen if ...?"- but Susan cut her off.

"I don't want to do this," she said flatly. Erin, a gifted and highly skilled facilitator, calmly countered by saying that while she understood that this wasn't a pleasant setting and she was sorry Susan was so uncomfortable, that she needed her to use that discomfort she was feeling and share what she was going through. She finally made a couple of contributions, but for the most part continued to refuse, repeating that she hated "this place". She simply checked out.

In that same exercise, there was another person who just couldn't shift from the dark future to the light one. She snapped at several of the other Futurists, then went on a tangent about US healthcare generally, and how the system as it stands is holding back human progress. Why didn't everyone admit that socialized medicine was the only civilized alternative, and let her deal with her patients as she saw fit? For her, everything came back down to that. She was challenging to work with because she couldn't break free of that framework, and didn't have any particular interest in doing so.

> *"I always give the people in my dark room small stress-relieving things to play with – rubber stress balls, putty, or tangle puzzles. This particular lady broke four of them during our session, which was a record. Clearly, she was pretty anxious."* - Erin

In the bright room, this person tried to take control of the discussion, and her obvious anger, carried over from the dark room, kept others from engaging. Sheryl smoothly regained control of the room by making everyone answer a simple question that made the future very personal to all of them: In the most optimistic future you can imagine, how do you feel about healthcare when you walk into your practice? This redirection to a personal view of an aspirational future broke the rather hostile dynamic and put the discussion back in Sheryl's control.

Another attendee who'd grown up in a repressive regime found the dark future too reminiscent of the pervasive sense of hopelessness she remembered from her childhood. It was all she could do to hold herself together. It took her a while to engage in the discussion, and she was definitely not one of the more vocal Futurists.

REACTIONS LIKE THESE, while not the norm, do happen – and

are another reason why it's essential to provide decompression time, space and activities when your people are moving between your Futuring rooms.

> *"As a facilitator, you have to be able to continue to reframe the questions in that room; to reengage people on an ongoing basis throughout the meeting. We are all human. You bring it back to them as individuals -what does this scenario mean to you?"* - Sheryl

> *"It's the opposite of collaboration, because whenever you as the facilitator come to a stumbling block, you go back to their personal feelings, or their personal fears, or their personal experiences."* - Erin

Another challenge is the person who wants to monopolize the discussion, or steer it back to their particular area of interest. Sometimes this is driven by ego; if they aren't working on it, how important can it be? Sometimes it's an emotional response, like that of the people described above, to some past experience that overwhelms them. Sometimes those Futurists who come from within your enterprise can try to pull rank, as it were, and declare themselves the de facto moderators. And more than once we've seen those whose work included private consultancies try to steer the discussion to the solutions their employers offered.

> *"When you're facilitating, there are times you have to be able to rein people in, or to step in and break up a discussion that's*

turning contentious. Sometimes there are two people that are really butting heads; you don't want to get too far down the rabbit hole, so you have to change your tactics as you go along."
- Sheryl

"*People get passionate, more often than you'd think. Under other circumstances — say, an advisory board — you could probably take all of the topics we discussed in the dark room and have a very civil, bland discussion around them, one that wouldn't move anyone, really. But because we're discussing these things in the Futuring context, every single person that came out of that meeting was affected by it in some way, positively or negatively. It created powerful, visceral responses - and that's exactly what you want to do, because the point is to get them thinking differently, seeing differently.*" - Erin

IT'S essential to your Futuring exercise that whoever is moderating it is experienced and expert enough at handling groups of people to defuse anger when it erupts, and to regain control of the room when someone highjacks it – and believe us, this will happen if you're not on top of it. While Futuring is in many ways a free-flowing discussion, it's useless for the purposes of problem solving if the Futurists are allowed to wander too far afield, or if individual contributions are shut down by one person. As a facilitator, be vigilant, and have some practiced strategies in place to keep the Futuring from going off the rails well before it commences.

Use the Wheel to keep them on task

Keeping people on task and out of the weeds is another challenge, and one for which we've developed a useful tool. During the exercise, we create a wall chart we call the Wheel; all around its perimeter are the various groups and subgroups that will be impacted by whichever future we're looking at, either light or dark, and chosen based on the environmental scan and the stakeholders. Every Wheel is customized and peopled differently, depending on the question we're working on, but typically in healthcare, the "spokes" could be patients, doctors, digital health, etc.

As we ask some of the standard questions we use in all of our healthcare Futuring sessions, we go around the Wheel and ensure we've discussed and included the attributes of this future from each of these stakeholders. All of them are intended to get to what the individual picturing herself or himself in this future is experiencing and feeling.

Not surprisingly in the healthcare realm, the dominant factor in the light future is usually the existence of universal access to healthcare – though there is not necessarily consensus in any group as to how this happens or should happen. In this bright future, these professionals see themselves as being able to work and serve to the best of their abilities, without financial or other constraints to prevent them from being effective.

Interestingly though, in one exercise, universal healthcare was also identified by those in the dark room as a negative:

> *"In the dark room vision of universal healthcare, healthcare is a right -but it's not good healthcare. There's no innovation, there's no R and D. It's not worth developing a medicine that is innovative or new because it won't be covered under the plan. That healthcare is driven by cost, not for the benefit of the patient. If you have a chronic disease, you're out of luck. We've lost so much expertise and innovation that if you want really good healthcare you have to leave the country. States even go to war, to keep each other's residents from crossing borders to use their healthcare systems." - Erin*

Next, we begin to drill down on the specific areas of interest on the spokes of the Wheel; those that have not been covered in the general conversation that's ensued. For instance, if one of the spokes is the payer environment and nobody in the group has addressed that, we talk about who pays for things in the future. We continue this part of the Futuring until all the spokes are discussed.

Using what you've learned

One of the great values of Futuring is uncovering the events that could cause a particular outcome, whether positive or negative. The animating question for this part of the conversation is "What might have made this outcome happen?" We call these events *drivers*.

In Erin's dark future, a major driver could be that the Affordable Care act was repealed and nothing replaced it, so that access to healthcare was severely curtailed. In Sheryl's bright future, the driver could be that data on the importance of preventive medicine had spurred the creation of a government policy to make preventive care available to all.

The appearance of these drivers can be spotted using what we call *signposts*; markers that someone who understands the possible outcomes to which they're pointing can spot ahead of that outcome actually occurring, and potentially act to mitigate. If you know that your car might one day refuse to start, for instance, and that one of the drivers of that could be that you're out of gas, a signpost that might allow you to reasonably foresee that outcome would be the little warning light popping up on your dashboard. If you see that light come on, you recognize not just the threat it presages – "My car is very likely to either not start, or to stop suddenly" – but also the opportunity that signpost presents to take action to prevent that from happening – "I'd better gas up the car."

The same things can pop up as positive or negative drivers, depending on how they're seen as playing out; big data is a good example. Clearly, we're living in a data-driven age, but our understanding of how that will actually affect our lives lags behind the technology for collection, and depending on who's got your data, you're either healthier, safer and better off, or left exposed and without protections for your privacy. Data collection in the bright future keeps us all healthier, allows us to track things like our immunization records easily and at a moment's notice, and means that no matter what ER in which we find ourselves unconscious, they'll be able to access everything they need to know about our health issues. But in the dark future, that kind of data could be used to deny us insurance; or, because it's not securely stored, anyone can steal it. The government uses it to make decisions about our worth; or it's never properly integrated into a universal system, so we can't manage or access our health records.

Even in the bright future there are disagreements about the desirability of a particular driver. For instance, in Pharma Alpha's Futuring, one person was talking animatedly about how great it would be when everyone is wearing some kind of health monitoring device that could help us meet our personal health and wellness goals. The medical ethicist in the room shook his head, and said, "I don't want some device pinging me day and night, or every time I eat a donut. That's an invasion of my privacy."

Seeing healthcare as a right rather than as a commodity was another driver, because the first view leads to universal health care, which was generally seen as a positive thing. And better educating everyone - from medical students to school children - about the benefits of healthy eating and the risks of elevate blood sugar was seen as another driver for Pharma Alpha.

"For Pharma Alpha, the cloud of ignorance and indifference to diabetes generally and specifically is a problem. That's a driver, so if the medical school curriculum doesn't change in

that direction, then nothing will change. There has to be some fundamental education about metabolic disease and its association with healthy aging in the medical school level, so that new doctors coming out know about it." - Erin

"We lined up all of the drivers that had been identified and had further conversations about them and what actions could be taken by Pharma Alpha to shift those drivers in a positive direction. What can we actually do to shift these drivers? What role can the company play? For instance, how could they best encourage medical schools to adopt that curriculum? The most direct and sensible route is talking to a prominent medical school, and getting them to model it. Then we talked about a new medical school that was opening; it might be easier to get them to add on to their curriculum." - Sheryl

"We used that as a jumping off point to brainstorm more ideas; someone from the company said, "We can't be the only ones at the table, but we could get a group together to fund a consortium of medical school directors and educate them about this issue. Creating that organization and getting people together could be our role." - Erin

For each of these drivers, the facilitator keeps pushing the participants to backtrack and look at not only the drivers, but also the opportunities they might contain – to intervene, for instance, in a way that might either support the positive drivers, or derail the negative ones. Whether the drivers themselves are positive or negative, what are the opportunities they might present? What actions could the company take, what partnerships might they need to form – with government, other agencies or professional associations, for instance – to be the most effective?

THE THING IS, if you're not nailing down an action plan that will help you to secure the bright future and/or cope with the challenges of a dark future, you're spinning your wheels. Futuring has to be relevant and actionable in order to have value. A skilled facilitator will relentlessly lead her Futurists back to that.

Key points for Chapter 10

1. A skilled facilitator is necessary to keep Futuring moving forward in a productive way.
2. Managing difficult personalities in the room - especially those who want to take over the discussion - requires tact and a firm hand.
3. Be aware that some Futurists can find the dark room experience deeply triggering and emotionally overwhelming.
4. Use the white wall to take down the insights and ideas generated during the Futuring.
5. Keep track of drivers and signposts identified during the Futuring, as well as the big ideas.

ELEVEN
MAKING SENSE OF THE FUTURE

It's tempting to want to finish the day up with everyone coming together to discuss the big ideas they've come up with through their Futuring experiences. You should, however, avoid this.

We did a session in which the Futurists all met at the end of the day, and most of them were too drained by the Futuring experience to do more heavy thinking. It's much better to wait until the next day, when everyone will have had a chance to rest and to further reflect on what they've discussed and heard. Even for the most creative, Futuring requires a big shift in thinking, and this one-day model, as good as it is, requires tremendous intellectual energy to get through. As we've seen, some people are going to find it emotionally draining too – and are more likely to withdraw into silence if they're obliged to continue while they're still processing the experience. Instead, let everyone go back to their rooms and relax, eat, or do whatever they like – and reconvene the following morning, when everyone's fresh.

At the end of the sessions, our small-group scribes take turns speaking to the larger group about the big ideas that came out in their respective light and dark sessions. Ideally, this happens the following morning, while everyone's together, now rested and refreshed after the previous long day of Futuring. While they talk, we're busy noting what they're saying on a graphic chart that shows what they've pinpointed as the big takeaways. This is a high-level presentation that's intended to prompt people's memories and get them seeing the connections. They then break out in groups to discuss the ideas that have been aired, and what needs to be done. If there's enough time, we can formulate initiatives; ideally, who would be involved in this, who are the stakeholders, and what would the timing be? This is framed around, "Here's where you'd really like to be: Here's where we think the drivers would be, so what are the gaps here? Can they best be addressed by private industry, by the government, or both? Who else should be involved, and why; academic institutions, religious institutions, the AMA? With whom does it make sense to partner?"

This takes a good two hours to do right, because it's important to identify the gaps properly. One that came up in Pharma Alpha's post-Futuring, for instance, was the lack of agreement in the medical world about the timing of treatment for the pre-diabetes state. One participant from the medical research side pointed out that early treatment is better, while the other side advocated only lifestyle changes until blood sugar reached particular levels. Parallels were drawn with statin treatment, especially in patients with normal or only slightly elevated cholesterol. Real scientific evidence supports either view; patients with abnormal blood sugar can be treated at any point usually without compromising their safety, but costs issues and the potential for long-term effects create valid arguments for waiting. There's a confusion about what is best, and clearly no consensus for these early stage patients.

These groups produce many ideas; at the end, we get everyone back together and prioritize those ideas into a top five list – then we all go to our individual rooms to put an action plan together in small groups, and ultimately, to reprioritize.

Some goals will have a clearer path to them than others, so the decision about what goals to concentrate on should not necessarily be based on just what's doable: It needs to be based on what would be the most impactful thing that could be done.

THAT LAST DISCUSSION of the day is what we as the facilitators will summarize, put into context, and deliver back to our client. We lay the results out for them in an actionable format we call the *Opportunity Map*: "Here are the things that you want to accomplish; here are the threats presented by the dark future, and the opportunities presented in the bright future; here is the list of signpost events to watch for that might indicate an important change in direction one way or the other. These are the prioritized actions in our bucket; here's a map of a collaborative approach and who needs to be on your team to pursue these goals going forward." It's detailed, in-depth, and specific, because it's a living document that's created to be used as a tool, not just a report to be stuck in a file and forgotten.

These post-Futuring meetings can also be done days after the event or even up to a couple of weeks afterward, if the logistics work for the Futurists. In the cases of Pharma Alpha and Pharma Beta, people had come from many locations, and that longer lag time wasn't possible.

Another way to go if your people are literally all over the map is using a virtual conference room; we've done that, too, and with good results. But however it's done, it's got to include all of your Futurists, and can't be too long after the event, because while a certain amount of time away from the Futuring gives people a chance to think into what they discussed, too much time risks them forgetting the details or ideas generated.

A final step for the meeting is creating a summary of the Futuring event. Summaries include the feelings expressed by the Futurists, the attributes of each future, the drivers for changes, signposts that allow environmental monitoring, and finally actual scenarios.

We create two scenarios for each future to illustrate the outcomes of the Futuring, in a story format that is easily understood by those who were not present at the session. A scenario is one or two paragraphs that tell the story of your future. Pharma Alpha's scenarios are presented below. The scenarios speak for themselves, but the first two present a dark future, while the second two show a desired future. The personalization of the narratives creates something much more memorable than bullets on a board.

Scenario 1: Loss of Faith in Science and Healthcare

A lack of governmental efforts to effectively integrate migrants has led to increasingly unstable societies across the globe, with some countries closing their borders completely. Inequality in all facets of life has become an acceptable consequence of the emerging environment and few efforts are made to resolve it, beyond a small core of protesters for whom the general public and governments alike have little tolerance. The political environment is particularly toxic, with a resistance to meaningful change and an over-focus on regulatory control, informed by corrupt policies designed to limit access to medicines, diminishing opportunities for innovation. Due to increasing nationalism, the ability for the large problems in science to be funded globally has all but disappeared. Initiatives to expand health innovation that flourished in the mid-2000s were reversed as governments deprioritized preventive policies in favor of short-term measures intended to control the immediate needs of their national constituents.

Inevitably, an increasing move to fully privatize all healthcare created a bigger engine to profit from the healthcare, and has resulted in a deep divide between the haves and have-nots, on both patient and HCP side. While the wealthy can still take advantage of privately funded research and innovative medicine, the impacts from a shrinking global intelligence and diminishing pool of physicians and scientists dedicated to health innovation has impacted every facet of society.

When polled, young and old across all countries say they feel unsupported, overwhelmed and highly anxious about healthcare, with little or no confidence that things will improve. Many wondered whatever happened to the promise of digital health, which held so many in thrall in the mid-2000s.

Scenario 2: Data Systems Collapse, Elderly Written Off

With the collapse of the data grid after the massive hack of 2022, the public and the healthcare community shunned attempts to re-establish digital health, largely based on fears for data security. In the ensuing disarray, the costs of healthcare skyrocketed, and prioritizations for access and treatments had to be made. Elder health was deprioritized and consequently, longevity trends over the last several decades are beginning to reverse.

Europeans are now living more and more of their later years with significant disease and disability. With reduced spending on social support for healthcare, a sense of hopelessness has taken hold, and since voluntary euthanasia became legal in many countries in the early 2020s, the number of elderly choosing this path in their final years has dramatically increased. For others, depression is a common and debilitating problem. Preventive medicine is completely out of reach for most of society but particularly for the elderly where the value is not appreciated. Care for patients with dementia is not prioritized within social health systems, and is far too costly for individuals to purchase through the growing private market. Age discrimination, despite being the focus of health report in the late 2010s, is now rampant in all walks of life.

Scenario 3: Live Long and Prosper

The increasing focus on preventive medicine across most European countries in the late 2010s, and early 2020s is beginning to pay off with a reduction in the number of over-65s with diabetes for the first time in over a decade. Obesity levels are also decreasing and despite the increase in lifespan of the average human, dementia rates have also stabilized.

Dramatic shifts in our understanding of the molecular basis for disease has resulted in truly personalized medicine for most common diseases. Strong collaboration between governments and private interests such as pharma and insurance, have facilitated a shift in public trust and a renewed support for science-based health. Digital health has become central to all lives and many people now contribute their health data to central data pools so that the promise of big data is finally being fulfilled. The commitment of the WHO and country commissions to age-friendly cities has extended to age-friendly health and wellness, with all individuals, regardless of age, having access to fulfilling work in the home or community, in an environment that is conducive to community support and holistic wellness. Lifespan is slowly increasing, but the number of healthy years lived as a percent of lifespan is increasing dramatically.

Scenario 4: Integrative Health Merges the Best of Everything

Healthcare and preventive care are thriving, with unprecedented efficiency in the healthcare system due to advances in technology and digital health. Digital triage has been remarkably successful, allowing patients to get the right care at the right time, from the right provider. Healthcare is viewed as a fully integrated service, with social and mental care administered alongside physical diagnosis and treatment, an outcome triggered by health policy changes after the migration crisis that peaked in 2021. Because of increased health efficiencies and access to digital health, every person has equal access to healthcare wherever they are located and at any time.

The elderly are among the biggest users of digital health after a cross-US effort to develop age-friendly tools, and to provide free education on how to use them. Across the lifespan, data and digital health have flourished, in large part because of large interdisciplinary collaborations across industries and governments, that have worked together to solve some of our biggest scientific and clinical challenges. Deep insights are being translated to practical care, such that the end of cancer is within sight, and many chronic diseases such as cardiometabolic disease or dementia are now able to be prevented or cured. When asked, individuals across most European countries say they feel optimistic and informed regarding their healthcare, and cite their confidence in good science as a key factor in their hopes for an even better future.

The use of dark scenarios allows us to consider how to best protect society against the bleak future they draw, with near-term actions. Typically, under each of these, both dark and light, we include a list of bullet points, that would include:

1. Implications to the business we are Futuring on, for each of these potential futures
2. The big idea we draw from each of these
3. What can we do now, to either help bring forward the bright future, or to mitigate the dark future?

IT'S important to remember in reviewing these and considering our potential to impact them going forward that the actual future is likely to be a combination of these scenarios; hence, the reason we have to maintain our focus on tracking indicators in the landscape moving forward, and adjusting course as needed. Scenarios that don't lead to action are just wheel-spinning, and that's not the purpose of this exercise.

Scenarios are invaluable in creating the sense of urgency about the future that can get you the support you need to continue on to the next steps. These next steps are all about how you bring the future into the present - and that's the topic of our final chapter.

Key points of Chapter 11

1. Expect your Futurists to be exhausted after this process, and give them time to return to their rooms and relax, ideally overnight, before reviewing the big ideas generated during the day.
2. At the end of the sessions, the group scribes take turns presenting the ideas generated in the dark and the light rooms.
3. Futurists break into groups to discuss the ideas that have been aired, and how to address them.
4. Afterward, prioritize those ideas into a "top five" list.
5. Create an action plan based on the threats and opportunities identified, and create a summary of the event.
6. Create at least two scenarios for each future, in an easy-to-understand story format.

TWELVE

KEEPING THE FUTURE PRESENT

SIGNPOST TRACKING, ONGOING ANALYSIS, AND COLLABORATORIES

Where does Futuring leave you – and what do you get out of it? The most valuable product of Futuring is the identification of those signposts that suggest a direction the present world is taking; movement which might be driving you toward either the brighter or the darker future. As you monitor them going forward, you're in a better position to connect the dots, and see where these trends or shifts are likely to come together to create change. So often humanity is caught flatfooted when what seems like an unpredictable Black Swan-type of event wallops us across the face: Meanwhile, Futurists are quietly plodding along, making the connections that enable them to see the shape of the future as it emerges.

We talked earlier about red herrings – those often much-heralded events that seem as though they're going to change the world, but fail to live up to their hype. Looking back at history, it's far commoner for a small thing that pops up, often unnoticed, to wind up being the big thing that really creates change. Red herrings in this context are attractive nuisances; they can look really cool, while distracting us from what matters.

> *"That's why it's so important, post-Futuring, to collect data on the things we see emerging; it gives us a leg up in deciding whether a given event is a genuine signpost or merely a red herring."* - Sheryl

---

Unless the people who are Futuring are committed to continuing to monitor the landscape, to meet regularly to discuss what they're seeing, and to use what they've learned to steer the corporate ship, the work has limited value. What's the use of creating scenarios, then going back to business as usual? Without scheduled follow-up built into your process, Futuring is a fascinating intellectual workout, seductive in itself but self-indulgent when not directed to change for the organization.

WHAT MIGHT KEEP you from continuing the necessary regular follow-up? One challenge in the business world (and certainly in the pharma world) is executive churn. If you're in healthcare, look around your C-suite or upper management and consider how long the people occupying those offices have been in their places - or how long they're likely to stay. Turnover is an issue, because tracking the drivers and spotting signposts requires continuity in monitoring the landscape - and without a champion in the organization who will make sure that the insights gained in Futuring aren't forgotten, it's too easy to lose sight of them. In the same vein, many leaders are hesitant to commit to longer-term Futuring, knowing that their company goals are short-term, and their current roles in the hierarchy likely to change.

Another roadblock to keeping the momentum going is that following up and monitoring isn't necessarily as intellectually stimulating as Futuring itself, and that the people you task with it, while they may initially be gung-ho, can lose steam pretty quickly when they're back in their regular seats and facing their already full plates of must-dos. The silo is real, people, and that sucking sound you hear are your colleagues being pulled back into theirs. Before long, meetings are being missed – and so are the signposts.

"Real life literally gets in the way. You're inspired, you are thinking about these things, you want to meet again with this person, and talk with that person, you've got an idea to do this and everything seems great and frenzied and "We are going to change the world" - then you come out and after just one day you've got 50 emails and 18 meetings to get to. It's back to reality and you don't have time for it." - Sheryl

---

We've solved this problem for some of our clients by creating what we call the Collaboratory; we feel it's really the best solution for not only following up on and growing the relationships and partnerships begun during the Futuring, but for keeping stakeholders focused on those outcomes going forward. Yes, as the person driving the decision to future on a topic with your colleagues and others, you need to have a sense of ownership – but internally there will always be competing priorities. The advantage of having an outside consultant is that they make sure it actually happens. For our clients, for instance, we organize the meetings, provide an agenda, and sit at the table to guide the conversation. We provide accountability.

Again, our involvement can be customized in terms of scale and frequency, depending on the problem you're faced with and how complex and long-term your response to it needs to be. But as the saying goes, "What isn't measured, isn't managed", and in this case the reverse is also true.

"The Collaboratory is the place to go when you see something happening that pertains to the futures you've explored. Sometimes that's just a matter of reporting on a positive development and tracking its impact. But when a signpost pops up that indicates a turn in a darker direction, that's a call to action, and the thinking needs to be, "We might need to do something: Is this an opportunity to be proactive, is it a chance to get ahead of some reactive thing we need to do?" There has to be a place for that conversation, and the Collaboratory plays a big part in keeping the future present." - Sheryl

"We set up quarterly meetings where we look at the signposts, enabling you to make decisions and act now, rather than react later. We help you to generate big ideas and we recommend when you should do another Futuring or take what you've come up with into a big idea forum. We get you reenergized and help you to keep it going, because unless someone's doing that, there's just not enough time in the day for a leader to carve this out over the long haul." - Erin

IF THE IDEA of hiring consultants to do this for your company isn't one you're willing to entertain, then you - as the internal champion of the process and the keeper of the results -have to be prepared to continue to take ownership of the follow-up over the long term. You can't delegate this duty to a couple of people whose job descriptions don't include it, and expect it to get done.

We suggest that a Collaboratory keep a constantly updated map of those signposts that marks when they show up, and where, whether they're red or green (and if they change) – and have a forum that meets at least four times a year, in which to discuss what you're seeing and what actions need to be taken to either nudge that signpost into the green or the red, depending on what kind of outcome it's pointing toward.

Key points for Chapter 12

1. Continual monitoring of trends and signposts is essential if your Futuring is to be fruitful going forward.
2. Executive churn can present a challenge in maintaining this continuity.
3. Another issue is that people don't find the process of monitoring as stimulating as the Futuring itself.
4. It's perilously easy to fall back into your silos and get caught up in day to day work.
5. A Collaboratory creates a solid structure to support continual monitoring of drivers and signposts as they appear, and allows you to consider what actions or projects must be delivered to keep your company moving toward the desirable future.

IN CLOSING

We hope that this overview of what we call Speed Futuring has been helpful to you, not only as a "how to" but more to the point, as a "why to".

We realize that it may be difficult to impossible for you to get your stakeholders on board for at least a five-year commitment to Futuring, or even a year-long one – although some companies in the healthcare space are already doing so, and honestly, your competitors may be among them. Speed Futuring lets you dip a toe in that stream, and bringing in our consultants and facilitators to run it makes it even more painless, and much less expensive.

As Futurists, we've participated in the multi-meeting, long-term model of Futuring, and while it's always interesting, in our experience spinning out lengthy scenarios sometimes leads you into the woods rather than out of them. Yes, there are benefits to that kind of long-term commitment – but those benefits are incremental. And while there's no comparison in terms of time invested and the costs incurred, the outcomes of these lengthy Futurings are very like those we get with Speed Futuring.

If you're in the business of coming up with big ideas and new projects, Speed Futuring can provide you with the rationale for supporting those, for instance. It allows you to build approval internally, provides you with strategic pillars that can guide your decision making, and puts up signposts you can actually track. That can lead to valuable new models of decision-making that are more company-wide and inclusive. One of our clients used their Speed Futuring as a springboard to launch exactly that kind of internal decision-making body to talk over projects that are bigger than any single silo, and which would affect the whole company. It's a shared thinking, it's a shared funding, and a shared risk model that wouldn't have happened had they not Futured with us first.

When we organize and develop a Speed Futuring for a client, we're flexible. We understand all the components and how they work, and we can take care of all of them or some of them for you, depending on your needs and preferences. For many clients, that means seeing us just three times ahead of the actual Futuring, with us providing the Futurists/experts, landscape assessment, doing the logistical planning and running the Futuring sessions, so that it's effectively a turnkey event. For others, that means simply coming in to run the Futuring sessions. It's a far more adaptive and customizable model than you'll find elsewhere. And frankly, as outsiders, it's easier for us to manage the big personalities in the room than it might be for you – particularly if they're part of your organization, or your boss.

What will you do with your future? Back at Shell where so much of what we do as industrial Futurists really began, their SKY scenario[1] paints a bold picture of a world and an industry taking charge of climate change, and meeting the goals of the Paris Climate Accord:

"SKY is an ambitious scenario to hold the increase in the global average temperature to well below 2°C. This requires a complex combination of mutually reinforcing drivers being rapidly accelerated by society, markets, and governments. From now to 2070 –

1. *A change in consumer mindset means that people preferentially choose low-carbon, high efficiency options to meet their energy service needs.*
2. *A step-change in the efficiency of energy use leads to gains above historical trends.*
3. *Carbon-pricing mechanisms are adopted by governments globally over the 2020s, leading to a meaningful cost of CO_2 embedded within consumer goods and services.*
4. *The rate of electrification of final energy more than triples, with global electricity generation reaching a level nearly five times today's level.*
5. *New energy sources grow up to fifty-fold, with primary energy from renewables eclipsing fossil fuels in the 2050s.*
6. *Some 10,000 large carbon capture and storage facilities are built, compared to fewer than 50 in operation in 2020.*
7. *Net-zero deforestation is achieved. In addition, an area the size of Brazil being reforested offers the possibility of limiting warming to 1.5°C, the ultimate ambition of the Paris Agreement."*

Clearly, Shell isn't letting the grass go under their feet, or leaving the outcomes to chance. They're heading the energy field as thought-leaders, actively engaging in shaping the future they want to see.

It's not hocus-pocus. It's not tea leaves. It's Futuring - *and it works.*

If you're intrigued by the potential Speed Futuring offers, we'd be happy to share our insights with you.

---

1. Shell Scenarios: SKY; Meeting the Goals of the Paris Agreement: https://www.shell.com/promos/meeting-the-goals-of-the-paris-agreement/_jcr_-content.stream/1530643931055/d5af41ae-f92d05d86a5cd77b3f3f5911f75c3a51c1961fe1c981daebda29b726/shellscenario-sky.pdf

ABOUT THE AUTHORS

Kelly Simpson, Founder, CSO, CEO of Simpson Healthcare and Chief Collaborative Officer at Summit Global Health began her career in Pharma as a Research Scientist at Pfizer. Her multi-award-winning company, Simpson Healthcare, is an established scientific agency whose employees provide the pharmaceutical, biotechnology, health technology, diagnostic and device industries with a wide range of disruptive solutions and content services in support of overall marketing strategies in health and disease.

Erin Conlan, Managing Director, Simpson Healthcare, began her career as a researcher at Pfizer in the Natural Products and Metabolism Laboratories. She departed research and development in search of a place where her expertise in biology, education, and communications could be better leveraged. She found a home at Simpson Healthcare, where for 20 years she has been focused on dissecting and simplifying the science, crafting compelling scientific narratives, and delivering that information to the right person at the right moment to evolve and humanize patient care. More recently, through her experience as a caregiver to a patient with a rare disease, she's developed a passion focused on ways to build health and impact wellness more broadly.

Sheryl Torr-Brown, PhD, SVP Medical, Simpson Healthcare, has diverse experience of the healthcare environment including research and development for Astra Zeneca, Searle, Monsanto and Pfizer, design innovation including pharmacy of the future with CVS/Caremark, and market research/product development for numerous healthcare offerings including devices for eye health and equine rehabilitation. At Simpson Healthcare, Sheryl is committed to exploration across boundaries, with a passion for deep innovation in medical strategy and the development of health-related content that moves people.

Made in the USA
Middletown, DE
05 March 2020